NEW PERSPECTIVES IN AMERICAN HISTORY

Donald B. Cole
The Phillips Exeter Academy
editor

Henry W. Bragdon
Samuel P. McCutchen
co-editors

THE ROAD TO INDEPENDENCE, 1763-1776
Benjamin W. Labaree

THE ORIGINS OF THE CONSTITUTION, 1776-1789
Francis L. Broderick

GOVERNMENT THROUGH OPPOSITION:
PARTY POLITICS IN THE 1790's
Frederick S. Allis, Jr.

THE HERO AND THE PEOPLE:
THE MEANING OF JACKSONIAN DEMOCRACY
Richard H. Brown

THE UNION DIVIDES: POLITICS AND SLAVERY,
1850-1861
Henry F. Bedford

THE PROGRESSIVE MOVEMENT: TRADITIONAL
REFORM
Albert C. Ganley

FROM IMPERIALISM TO ISOLATIONISM, 1898-1919
Ernest R. May

THE NEW DEAL: INTERPRETATIONS
Wallace E. Davies

FROM VERSAILLES TO NUREMBERG: THE
AMERICAN ENCOUNTER WITH THE NAZIS
Henry F. Bedford

THE UNITED STATES AND LATIN AMERICA,
1933-1968: FROM THE GOOD NEIGHBOR POLICY
TO THE ALLIANCE FOR PROGRESS
Harold A. Bierck

RECONSTRUCTION AND THE AMERICAN NEGRO,
1865-1900
Francis L. Broderick

THE MAKING OF INDUSTRIAL AMERICA, 1840-1900
William Greenleaf

U. S. POLICIES TOWARD CHINA
Paul S. Holbo

NOBODY KNOWS: BLACK AMERICANS IN THE
TWENTIETH CENTURY
David Tyack

New Perspectives in American History

THE COLD WAR

ROBIN W. WINKS
Yale University

DANIEL YERGIN
Harvard University

Macmillan Publishing Co., Inc.
New York
Collier Macmillan Publishers
London

Earlier edition *THE COLD WAR: From Yalta to Cuba* by Robin W.
Winks, © Copyright Macmillan Publishing Co., Inc. 1964

ACKNOWLEDGMENTS

For permission to quote copyright material, the authors are grateful to
the following:

Simon & Schuster, Inc., New York, for the excerpts on pages 15-16,
from *Atomic Diplomacy* by Gar Alperovitz, copyright 1970.

Macmillan Publishing Co., New York, for the excerpts on pages 16-17,
from *War and Politics* by Bernard Brodie, copyright 1973.

Random House, Inc., New York, for the excerpts on page 71, from
The Arrogance of Power by J. William Fulbright, copyright 1966.

Cassell & Company, Ltd., London, for the excerpts on page 24, from
The Diaries of Sir Alexander Cadogan by David Dilks, copyright 1972.

Macmillan Publishing Co., Inc.
866 Third Avenue
New York, N.Y. 10022
Collier Macmillan Canada, Ltd.

ISBN 0-02-244190-5

Printed in the United States of America

Text design: Katherine B. Stevens

Contents

JOURNEY TO PEKING   1

THE BREAKUP OF AN ALLIANCE   3

A NEW WAR BEGINS   18

NO PEACE FOR ASIA   38

STANDOFF IN EUROPE
AND THE MIDDLE EAST   52

CONFRONTATION IN
LATIN AMERICA   62

VIETNAM AND THE DOMINO THEORY   74

"DETENTE"   95

JOURNEY TO PEKING

Peking, the capital of the People's Republic of China, has always been known as "The Forbidden City." In 1949 it became especially forbidden to Americans. In that year, Communist guerrillas defeated the Nationalist forces, ending a long and bitter civil war. For the next twenty-two years, the United States, the most powerful nation in the world, and China, the most populous, were locked in bitter hostility. The two countries did not recognize each other. They did not carry on diplomatic contacts.

That situation came to an end on February 20, 1972, when a 707 jet called "The Spirit of '76" appeared over the Forbidden City. Though American, this jet was welcome. Once on the ground, the plane's door swung open, revealing a figure that hesitated for a moment. Then Richard Nixon, President of the United States, walked down the steps and shook hands with the Premier of China, Chou En-lai. There followed eight days of intimate conversations between the American delegation and top Chinese officials. The high point of this visit came when Mao Tse-tung, known to most of the world as more of a legend than as a real person, received the President in his private library.

The leaders on both sides knew they were at a turning point. One period of history was ending, and another was beginning. President Nixon's journey to Peking – and the one he took a few months later to a similar summit in the Russian capital of Moscow — were major steps on the long march away from the sharp division between "West" and "East," between "free world" and "Communist world." For a quarter century, people had called that confrontation between the two blocs the "Cold War." Yet even as President Nixon and Mao Tse-tung talked in Peking, the war in Vietnam — the tragic child of the Cold War — still raged on. And so, even if those summit meetings did signal a turning point, it would take more than a week to turn the corner between eras.

The Cold War, which began in the rubble of Europe after World War II and finally played its closing act in the jungles and rice paddies of Indochina in the early 1970's, was a period when peace was impossible and total war improbable. It was an age of permanent anxiety. Political scientists described it as a "zero-sum" game — a win for one side was an automatic loss for the other. And each side feared that any loss, no matter how small, could lead to total defeat. Misunderstanding was easy in such an atmosphere, and it was almost inevitable that spies and traitors were sometimes imagined when they did not exist. Indeed, even if Russia and America were not willing to go to total war, they would use almost any other means to compete. Not only foreign aid but even the race to the moon and children's reading ability played a role in the Cold War. Moreover, America and Russia moved dangerously close to the brink on several occasions. There were many confrontations — over Greece in 1947, Berlin in 1949, and Cuba in 1962, to name three — and two fierce "limited wars" in Korea and in Vietnam. And every person lived with the terrible daily threat of nuclear war — a war after which, said a Russian leader, "the living would envy the dead."

How and why did the Cold War start? Why did it develop the way it did? Why, for a quarter century after World War II, did the United States not secure the "businesslike relations" it finally developed with Russia and China in 1972? And what connection could there be between events in Poland in the 1940's and events half way round the world in Vietnam in the 1970's?

In many ways, the story of the Cold War begins with a trip by another American President to a summit in another Communist country at another time.

THE BREAKUP
OF AN ALLIANCE

On February 3, 1945, a four-engine Skymaster, large by the standards of its time but tiny compared to today's jumbo jets, landed at the city of Saki in Soviet Russia. Its most important passenger was the President of the United States, Franklin D. Roosevelt. On his arrival, a Red Army band played "The Star-Spangled Banner." Then the President was helped to a car, for a six-hour, ninety-mile drive over winding mountain roads to the Black Sea resort of Yalta. There, in the ballroom of the Czar's former summer palace (turned into a resort for working people in 1925), he met for seven days with Soviet leader Joseph Stalin and Britain's Prime Minister Winston Churchill. With victory in sight both in Europe and in the Pacific, the three men talked not only about war strategy but also about the shape of the world after the end of World War II.

The conference was historic, for it was both the high tide of allied unity in World War II and the first scene in the Cold War. The roots of the Cold War lay in the great changes brought about by the war that began in 1939 and ended in 1945. England, though one of the victors, was greatly weakened; much of its economic vitality had been drained away by the costs of war. Japan and Germany were reduced to rubble, as was much of the rest of Europe. In consequence, the two Superpowers, the United States and the Soviet Union, neither of which were experienced in world leadership, stood eyeing each other nervously across the wreckage of war.

The Grand Alliance in World War II, connected only by common opposition to Hitler, was composed of unlikely partners. The United States—many of its citizens disillusioned by the failure of Woodrow Wilson's crusade to "make the world safe for democracy"—had been resolutely isolationist between the two wars. In particular, Americans wanted to keep the nation away from what Ernest Hemingway called "the hell broth brewing" in Europe in the 1930's. Many agreed with Senator Robert Taft of Ohio, a leading isolationist, that the United States could go it alone: "My whole idea of foreign policy is based largely on the position that America can successfully defend itself against the rest of the world."

The Soviet Union had also been isolationist until a few years before World War II, partly because its dictator, Joseph Stalin, was preoccupied with "building socialism in one country." In addition, European states isolated Russia because they considered communism a threat to their own social orders. In the late 1930's, England and France explored the possibility of forming an alliance with the Soviet Union to restrain Adolph Hitler's Germany. But the effort failed. After the Munich Crisis of 1938 when Hitler gained partial control of Czechoslovakia, Stalin became convinced that France and England were trying to turn Hitler eastward—toward the Soviet Union. Meanwhile, the Western countries began to have doubts about the Soviet Union as a reliable ally. Their doubts were increased by the cataclysmic purge of the leadership in the Soviet Union, which Stalin had ordered.

Stalin wanted time to build up the Red Army. He wanted to keep the Soviet Union out of war as long as possible. He wanted to find a way to turn Hitler's ambitions back toward Western Europe. Thus on August 23, 1939, he signed a dramatic and unexpected nonaggression pact with the bitterly anti-Communist Hitler. Then on September 1, Hitler invaded Poland, which brought England and France, Poland's allies, into war against Germany, but not Russia. This invasion was the beginning of World War II.

The Nazi-Soviet Pact made the Soviet Union's relations with the West even more difficult. The two dictators, Stalin and Hitler, seemed to be cut from the same pattern—a pattern that was being defined as *totalitarianism.*

The entire situation changed in June 1941. Nazi troops had already overrun most of Europe and were at the English Channel, seemingly prepared for a knock-out strike against Great Britain. But Hitler, bloated with success and his appetite for conquest still unsatisfied, could not contain his ambitions. To the East was the Soviet Union, still Germany's great rival. And so, in the early morning hours of June 22, 1941, Hitler threw his armies into a lightning attack on the Soviet Union. In this way, he notified the Soviets that he was canceling the Nazi-Soviet Pact. Stalin was caught by surprise; he had trusted his fellow dictator too much. The Red Army fell back helplessly against the powerful German invaders.

For the three countries that would make up the Grand Alliance, the situation was desperate. Great Britain was standing alone at the edge of Europe; it had already suffered heavily under the furious air war called the Battle of Britain. Under the Lend-Lease Act of March 1941, America began sending supplies to Great Britain. But American leaders suspected that it was only a matter of time before the United States would be forced to enter both the European war and the war Japan was fighting in the Far East. Then America would need allies. Russia, reeling under the German invasion, most certainly needed the help of Western countries. For the West, the German invasion was a godsend. "It will mean," Roosevelt wrote a friend, "the liberation of Europe from Nazi domination—and at the same time I do not think we need worry about any possibility of Russian domination." Churchill did not hide his feelings when he told the House of Commons: "I would ally myself with the devil himself if it would help me defeat the Nazis." The United States and Great Britain began sending aid to Russia shortly after the German invasion.

On December 7, 1941, Japanese planes suddenly appeared over Pearl Harbor and bombed United States naval forces there. The United States declared war on Japan. In those dark days when the Axis powers—Nazi Germany, Fascist Italy, and Japan—seemed to be on the offensive in every part of the world, the Grand Alliance began to take shape.

Among the Allies, the United States did most of the fighting in the Far East, but even the American strategists agreed that the war in Europe was more important. Churchill and Roosevelt, remembering the terrible losses in trench warfare in World War I, were reluctant to make an immediate attack on the Nazi armies defending "fortress Europe." The Russians, however, engaged in a life-and-death struggle on their own soil, had no such choice. They bore the bulk of casualties — more than twenty million dead and millions more wounded and crippled. The Americans organized their economy to produce the bulk of war material, of which eleven billion dollars' worth went to the Russians as lend-lease.

The tide of war turned in 1943, as the Allies took the offensive. With success on the battlefield, the Allies could now began to think about the postwar world. Roosevelt, like President Woodrow Wilson a generation before, hoped that the war could be followed by "a better world, an ordered world." But Roosevelt, who had been Wilson's Assistant Secretary of the Navy, wanted to avoid Wilson's mistakes. One mistake had been lack of preparation for peace. The tempo before the Versailles Peace Conference following World War I, said Roosevelt, had been like that "of the lady who is told at noon that she is to accompany her husband on a month's trip on the three o'clock train that afternoon." Roosevelt wanted to establish, during wartime, the basis for a realistic postwar collaboration among the Allies. The alternative, he feared, was another arms race — and another war. He thought that Wilson and other idealistic Americans had ignored "the factor of power" in trying to make peace. In Roosevelt's mind, the only way to prevent another war was to make a settlement guaranteed by the great powers. "We must have a brand new approach to world peace," the President told visiting Soviet Foreign Minister Molotov in 1942. "The old balance of power theory did not work." The Four Policemen — as Roosevelt dubbed the big four (U.S., Britain, Russia, China) — "would maintain sufficient armed force to impose peace" after the war. "The population of our nations and friends was well over a billion people," Roosevelt said. "We at least could be sure of the peace for twenty-five years; at any rate until all of us now living are dead."

The British and Americans generally agreed to postwar goals for a liberal world order, with self-determination for the peoples of Europe. There were some differences. The Americans were suspicious of "British imperialism"; they mistakenly thought that Great Britain would emerge from the war with a powerful economy, intent on staking out new markets and raw materials. The British, on the other hand, felt that the Americans were forcing "subservience" on them, as Foreign Secretary Anthony Eden put it. In particular, the British thought that the Americans were trying to reduce the British role in world trade, which was the lifeblood of the English economy. It was true that the Americans had detailed plans for reforming the world economy in ways that would benefit the United States. But the Americans also believed that their plans would benefit all nations.

Despite such differences, however, relations between the two countries were close, cemented at the top by the friendship that developed between President Roosevelt and Prime Minister Churchill. "Winston will, I think, settle down in the U.S.!" one British diplomat noted half-jokingly during a Churchill visit to the White House. The Prime Minister, the diplomat added, "talks with the President until 2 A.M. and constantly spends a large part of the day hurling himself violently in and out of bed, bathing at unsuitable moments and rushing up and down corridors in his dressing gown."

The big powers scheme also appealed to Joseph Stalin, the suspicious Soviet leader whom Roosevelt met for the first time in 1943 at the Tehran Conference. Stalin was a short, stocky man from Soviet Georgia, where many years before he had been a seminary student before becoming an underground revolutionary. One diplomat thought that with his black hair swept back, he looked like a porcupine. He was simple and flat in his speech, and would absentmindedly doodle wolves while discussing affairs of state. The unchallenged leader of the Soviet Union, he was associated with the doctrine of "socialism in one country." Unlike other Communists such as his old rival Leon Trotsky, Stalin was more interested in developing communism inside the Soviet Union than in making a world revolution. He was dedicated to building Russia up into a major—or the major—industrial power in the world. In the course of reaching that goal, he resorted to terror, purges, prison camps, and mass executions. Although Stalin was the leading Communist in the world, he often acted like a twentieth-century czar. Idealistic programs like the Atlantic Charter (a declaration of peace aims which Churchill and Roosevelt had conceived at a meeting in August 1941) were of little interest to him. "A declaration I regard as algebra, but an agreement as practical arithmetic," he said. "I prefer practical arithmetic." Therefore, when he met Roosevelt at Tehran, he made it clear that he would accept an international organization only if the real power would remain with the great powers.

One of Roosevelt's political problems was to get Stalin to remain in a coalition of great powers after the war. Another problem was to win the American people over to supporting a leading role for the United States in world affairs. Once the Japanese attack on Pearl Harbor had shown the American people that isolationism would no longer work, the second problem became far less difficult. Toward the end of the war, Republican Senator Arthur Vandenberg, in effect, summarized the great change in American thinking when he "confessed" that his own earlier isolationism had been a mistake:

> I have always been frankly one of those who has believed in our own self-reliance. . . . But I do not believe that any nation hereafter can immunize itself by its own exclusive action. . . . I want maximum American cooperation, consistent with legitimate American self-interest, with constitutional processes and with collateral events which warrant it, to make the basic idea of Dumbarton Oaks [the United Nations plan] succeed. I want a new dignity and a new authority for international law.

But public opinion still rested on the same kind of idealistic premises that had supported first Wilson's crusade for a world organization (the League of Nations) following World War I and then the isolationism of the 1920's. Phrases like "big powers" and "spheres of influence" were considered dirty words. Secretary of State Cordell Hull was addressing this public opinion when he told the Senate after he had returned from attending the Moscow Conference in late 1943, where the Four Powers had declared themselves in favor of establishing a United Nations organization: "There will no longer be need for spheres of influence, for alliances, for balance of power, or any other of the arrangements through which, in the unhappy past, the nations strove to safeguard their security or to promote their interests." It was crucial that the Senate support the plans for an international organization because, under the Constitution, it had to approve all treaties. Senate opposition had prevented United States participation in the League of Nations after World War I.

Roosevelt, moving more slowly than many members of his administration, finally endorsed a postwar United Nations. To Stalin he made it clear, however, that this endorsement would depend on the big powers. Roosevelt did not make this condition clear to the American public for he was afraid that if he did, the entire movement to bring public opinion around to supporting international cooperation would collapse. Stalin certainly never took the United Nations seriously. He was more interested in securing border changes and in getting goods and equipment from Germany to help rebuild a devastated Russia than in participating in what Senator Vandenberg called "the town meeting of the world."

The Yalta Conference had been preceded by both ominous and hopeful signs. An ominous sign was that on January 5, 1945, the Soviet Union had gone ahead and recognized the pro-Communist Lublin Committee as the government of Poland instead of the anti-Soviet Polish government exiled in London, which was recognized by both Britain and the United States. Yet, just a week later when the Germans launched a furious counterattack in the West — the Battle of the Bulge — that threatened the destruction of the Allied forces, Stalin hurriedly launched an offensive against the Germans in the East. At Yalta, Stalin gruffly turned away the fulsome thanks of both Churchill and Roosevelt. The Russians had staged their offensive early, he said, "because they felt it to be their duty as Allies."

There was a heady atmosphere at Yalta, for the three leaders were redrawing the map of the world. Roosevelt and Churchill made a series of bargains with Stalin that were later criticized. The Americans wanted Russian participation in the Pacific war, and Stalin promised to enter that war three months after the fighting ended in Europe. In return, the Soviets would receive, after victory, Japan's Kurile Islands and the southern half of Sakhalin Island that Russia had ceded to Japan in 1905. The Soviets would also regain control over the Manchurian ports of Dairen and Port Arthur. (Japan had seized Manchuria from the Chinese in 1931 and ran it as the puppet state of Manchukuo.) It was also agreed that a joint Soviet-Chinese group would operate the railway system in Manchuria, which would be restored to China at the end of the war, after Japan was defeated.

A compromise was reached on the new United Nations. The permanent members of the Security Council, who would be the big powers, would have a veto over any substantive action taken by the United Nations, although they would not be able to prevent discussion. The leaders also agreed that a conference to draw up a United Nations charter, based on an American draft, would open in San Francisco on April 25, 1945.

Churchill and Roosevelt won Stalin's agreement to a "Declaration on Liberated Europe," which promised free elections in all the countries that had been under Nazi control. The only problem was that the declaration was unenforceable. Roosevelt acknowledged that only by another war could the Soviet sphere of influence be upset in Eastern Europe. But Stalin again made it clear that he was really only interested in a big powers peace. "The main thing was to prevent quarrels in the future between the three great powers," he told Churchill and Roosevelt. "The greatest danger was a conflict between the three great powers."

The two most difficult questions at the Yalta Conference dealt with the heart of Europe — Germany and Poland. The Russians insisted that Germany be broken into smaller states, as it had been before 1870, so that it could not again rise to challenge the peace. In pushing this plan, Stalin was only reworking a proposal of Roosevelt's from the Tehran Conference. But Russia's fear of a renewed Germany was far greater than that of the West. For Stalin knew that, during World War I, one German offensive had helped to topple Czarist Russia and that a second attack in World War II had almost wiped out Soviet Russia. The conference agreed to "dismember" Germany into a group of smaller states. The Russians also wanted reparations — goods and equipment from Germany to make up for what had been destroyed in the war. Roosevelt agreed to a tentative figure of $20 billion, half to go to the Soviet Union, while Churchill, worried about the economic consequences for the rest of Europe, straddled the fence. The details were left to a joint international commission that would meet later in Moscow.

Poland was the first Cold War "question" to cause a rift between the Allies. Each of the Allies saw Poland as a test of the other's sincerity, and each ultimately saw it as a betrayal. Since the days of Peter the Great, Russian policy had been concerned with the approaches to Russia through Poland. "Throughout history, Poland has always been a corridor for attacks on Russia," Stalin said at Yalta. "During the last thirty years, our German enemy has passed through this corridor twice." One of the war aims of Russia, therefore, had been control of Poland or the establishment of a regime that could be counted on to be friendly to Russia. During the latter part of the war, the Lublin Committee had played this role. At Yalta, the Allies agreed that a Polish Provisional Government of National Unity was to be set up, including leaders from both the Lublin Committee and the anti-Soviet London Polish government, and "free and unfettered elections as soon as possible" were promised. The Soviet Union took some of Poland's eastern territory, and Poland, in turn, was compensated with parts of eastern Germany.

All sides were pleased with the agreements at Yalta. The Russians called the unseasonably warm weather "Roosevelt weather" to honor the spirit of accord. "As long as Stalin lasted, Anglo-Russian friendship could be maintained," Churchill told some members of Parliament a few days later. The American delegation was delighted. Harry Hopkins, Roosevelt's special assistant for foreign policy, later recalled: "We really believed in our hearts that this was the dawn of the new day we had all been praying for and talking about for so many years. . . . The Russians had proved that they could be reasonable and far-seeing, and there wasn't any doubt in the minds of the President or any of us that we could live with them and get along with them peacefully for as far into the future as any of us could imagine." Yet everything would depend on how the agreements were interpreted and put into effect. And so the reaction had to be tentative. Roosevelt caught this uncertain note in a letter he scribbled to his wife on his last day at Yalta: "We have wound up the conference — successfully, I think."

Events rushed by at dizzying speeds in the next few months. And difficulties set in. The Western governments and the Soviet Union could not agree on how to set up a Polish Provisional Government. Moreover, American and British leaders were deeply disturbed by the unilateral and high-handed efforts of the Soviets to extend their control over other governments in Eastern Europe — in what was seen as violations of the Yalta "Declaration on Liberated Europe." The Russians, in turn, were aroused to great suspicion by the efforts of Allen Dulles, later director of the Central Intelligence Agency, to arrange an armistice with German troops in Northern Italy. The Russians feared that these efforts would lead, perhaps, to a separate surrender in the West, which would free more Nazi troops to fight Russia in the East. Their ill-tempered complaints deeply stung Roosevelt.

Both British and American leaders emphasized in the days after Yalta that everything depended on Stalin's survival. But Stalin was not the first to go. In the midst of all the difficult diplomatic problems, Franklin Roosevelt, while sitting for his portrait on April 12, 1945, complained of a terrible headache and collapsed. A few hours later, he was dead. The new President of the United States, Harry S Truman, was unknown. He had been chosen as the vice-presidential candidate in 1944 chiefly to keep the liberal Henry Wallace, former Secretary of Agriculture and then still Vice-President, off the ticket. The widespread grief and mourning for Roosevelt was interrupted by nervous jokes about the former haberdasher from Kansas City, who was now in the White House. Truman seemed as doubtful about himself as the nation was. In his memoirs, he recalled his first meeting with reporters, after being sworn into office:

> "Boys," I said, "if you ever pray, pray for me now. I don't know whether you fellows ever had a load of hay fall on you, but when they told me yesterday what had happened, I felt like the moon, the stars, and all the planets had fallen on me."
> "Good luck, Mr. President," said one of the reporters.
> "I wish you didn't have to call me that," I told him.

Indeed, it did seem as though the moon, the stars, and all the planets had fallen on Truman. He had not participated in making Roosevelt's policies, nor had he been informed of them. Now all kinds of problems awaited his decision; many of them were also unfamiliar to others in the government.

In the second week of May 1945, German resistance collapsed. The war in Europe was now over. Hitler's Reich, which he had boasted would last a thousand years, had barely lasted twelve.

One of Truman's first decisions was to go ahead with the long-awaited conference to establish an organization to ensure world peace — the United Nations. From April to June, representatives of the victorious Allies, filled with a sense of historic mission, met in San Francisco and framed a charter for the United Nations. A bipartisan delegation from the United States rallied public support for the new organization. Arthur Vandenberg, the former isolationist Republican, used his influence to convince others in the United States Senate of the importance of the United Nations. The United States could best make its moral weight and its strength felt by joining and, indeed, by leading the new organization, he argued.

Although the Senate in 1919 had dramatically rejected Wilson's League of Nations, the United Nations charter swept through the Senate in 1945 with only two dissenting votes — so much had public opinion changed. The plan for this new organization, primarily American, incorporated the agreements made at Yalta. The Security Council, more important than the General Assembly, had five permanent members — Roosevelt's Four Policemen (United States, the United Kingdom, Union of Soviet Socialist Republics, and China) plus France — and six other states on a rotating basis. The permanent members had the veto, which all the great powers agreed was necessary to protect their sovereignty.

Truman's other early decision was to take a harder line with the Russians. Truman did not "expect one hundred percent of what we proposed," he said, but he did think "we should be able to get eighty-five percent." If the Russians did not want to cooperate with the United States at the United Nations and elsewhere, "they could go to hell." He gave visiting Russian Foreign Minister Molotov a dressing down, in which he told the Russian how disturbed the United States was by the Soviet refusal to accept the Western interpretation of the Polish agreement.

"I have never been talked to like that in my life," Molotov said stiffly.

"Carry out your agreements and you won't get talked to like that," the President snapped back.

Although the two countries seemed headed for a collision, the United States was doing nothing to prepare for it. Demobilization of American troops in Europe began almost immediately after the surrender of Germany on May 7, 1945. The very next day, May 8, Truman signed an order—without reading it—abruptly reducing lend-lease supplies to the Allies, including the Soviet Union, at a time when the Allies' wartime economies were still geared to such aid. Without warning, most of the aid ceased. Some ships turned back in midvoyage. The Russians, always doubtful of the West, viewed this order as a betrayal, since they had pledged to enter the Pacific war. Truman later described this order as one of his first major mistakes. Three months later, after the end of the Pacific war, Truman further terminated all other aid to the Allies, prompting Churchill to remark that he hoped Americans would not "proceed in such a rough and harsh manner as to hamper a faithful ally—an ally who had held the fort while their own armaments were prepared."

But the tensions of April and May receded. The atmosphere became calmer, though tension was still in the air when in mid-July, Truman, Churchill, and Stalin met in Potsdam, a suburb of ruined Berlin that had been a favorite residence of the German film colony. Here the three leaders worked on the foundations for peace. They created a Council of Foreign Ministers, and they agreed on three D's—to de-Nazify, demilitarize, and democratize Germany. Each occupying power (Great Britain, United States, Union of Soviet Socialist Republics, and France) was authorized to take property from its German zone of occupation, as reparations. A control council of the four nations would decide on matters relating to Germany as a whole. Boundaries between the zones were determined, and Berlin was to lie 110 miles inside the Soviet zone, although each power was to occupy a section of the city itself.

Unlike Roosevelt, Harry Truman did not glory in the give-and-take of negotiations, and he was often impatient at the Potsdam Conference. But partway through the meeting, Churchill noted a new confidence and assurance in the President. Truman had just learned that a test atomic bomb had been exploded over the white sands of New Mexico. After one conference session, the President strolled over to Stalin and told him that the United States had this powerful new weapon. "Good," replied Stalin, adding that he hoped "the Americans would use it." In fact, it is almost certain that Stalin already knew about the weapon through Russia's espionage sources.

The Americans wasted no time in using it, despite the concern of scientists like Albert Einstein, who realized how terrible a weapon it was. On August 6, 1945, an American plane slipped down over Hiroshima and released a single bomb. Some 71,000 people were killed in the explosion. The bomb was, by far, the most powerful weapon ever known to man. Two days after the bombing of Hiroshima, Russia honored her bargain at Yalta (and with good reason, since she hoped for major territorial gains from the defeat of Japan) and entered the war by invading the Chinese province of Manchuria, then occupied by the Japanese. The next day the United States dropped a second atomic bomb on the city of Nagasaki. On August 14, President Truman read a message to the American people: Japan had surrendered unconditionally.

The decision to drop the atomic bomb has come to be one of the most controversial of all American foreign-policy decisions. Gar Alperovitz, in *Atomic Diplomacy,* argues that the bomb was not necessary militarily, but was used primarily because of problems in America's relations with the Russians.

> . . . [T]he decision to use the weapon did not derive from overriding military considerations. Despite Truman's subsequent statement that the weapon "saved millions of lives," Eisenhower's judgment that it was "completely unnecessary" as a measure to save lives was almost certainly correct. . . .
>
> [B]efore the atomic bomb was dropped each of the Joint Chiefs of Staff advised that it was highly likely that Japan could be forced to surrender "unconditionally," without use of the bomb and without an invasion. . . .
>
> Political considerations related to Russia played a major

role in the decision; from at least mid-May, American policymakers hoped to end the hostilities before the Red Army entered Manchuria. For this reason, they had no wish to test whether Russian entry into the world would force capitulation—as most thought likely—long before the scheduled November invasion. Indeed, they actively attempted to delay Stalin's declaration of war. . . . [T]he second of the two overriding considerations seems to have been that combat demonstration was needed to convice the Russians to accept the American plan for a stable peace. And the crucial point of this effort was the need to force agreement on the main questions in dispute: the American proposals for Central and Eastern Europe. President Truman may well have expressed the key consideration in October 1945. . . . [T]he President declared: "It is only by strength that we can impress the fact upon possible future aggressors that we will tolerate no threat to peace."

The Alperovitz thesis has been challenged by Bernard Brodie, one of America's most distinguished strategists, who more convincingly argues in his book *War and Politics* that military considerations did indeed determine the decision to use the bomb:

> Our military chieftains expected their planned invasion to be extremely costly in lives, and our present knowledge gives us no reason to assume they were exaggerating. . . .
> But were the two nuclear weapons necessary? . . . Would the same effect have been accomplished by the demonstration urged by a group among the scientists who had produced the bomb? . . .
> A demonstration over a deserted island would have been anything but impressive, and there were too few bombs in hand to use one in that manner. . . .
> The two bombs heightened the Emperor's determination to end the war as soon as possible. Several cabinet ministers, affected the same way, moreover felt that they now had a powerful new leverage for persuading the Army diehards in and out of the cabinet to acquiesce in a surrender. . . .
> Lately a typically "revisionist" kind of speculation has developed to the effect that the government really wanted to impress was not so much that of Japan as that of the Soviet Union. It is impossible to hold that the thought never crossed the minds of the President or his advisors. What

we can say, however, is that to the extent that it did cross their minds, it could not have been a critical consideration. It seems not to have been mentioned in the relevant councils, and the people pondering the question apparently found quite enough incentive for using the bomb in their great desire to end as quickly as possible the war with Japan. Moreover, at that time the Cold War had not yet begun to throw its chill upon the relations between the two Superpowers.

In truth, there was good reason to think that the Japanese would have made a last, fight-to-the-death stand against the United States. Japanese military leaders would have considered surrender a great humiliation. Thus, the atomic bomb may well have saved not only hundreds of thousands of American lives but also hundreds of thousands, if not millions, of Japanese lives that would have been lost by an invasion.

A NEW WAR BEGINS

The atomic bomb seemed to change everything. Nation states had to recalculate all their equations of power. How many tens or hundreds of thousands of infantry were now equal to one of these new weapons? No one in this time of rapid, confusing change knew how to compute this new math. But it was clear that the role of the United Nations was now more uncertain. E. B. White, of *The New Yorker,* caught the mood when he wrote: "The preparations made at San Francisco for a security league of sovereign states to prevent aggression now seem like the preparations some little girls might make for a lawn party as a thunderhead gathers just beyond the garden gate. The lemonade will be spiked by lightning. The little girls will be dispersed. Nuclear energy and foreign policy cannot co-exist on the planet."

Foreign policy could not be abolished. Nations still had to order their relations with other nations. But the relations between the United States and the Soviet Union took on a special character. The postwar world became a *bipolar* world. That is, it divided into two hostile blocs led by two Superpowers — the United States and the Soviet Union. There have been other periods in history when powerful states led opposing coalitions. But the bipolarity of the Cold War was intensified by the fact that the United States and the Soviet

Union not only opposed each other as two rival nation-states, they also represented two very different ideologies. The differences have to do with the basic beliefs and values around which the two societies are organized.

The United States was born of an 18th-century revolution—a liberal revolution. Five legacies of that revolution still help to shape America's basic outlook in world affairs. First is the principle that people are free to think for themselves and to make up their own minds. In our system people are guaranteed certain basic rights of expression and political organization. We are protected against the arbitrary acts of others, be they private groups or the government, by a series of judicial processes. Second, our system of government is based on representation. The people choose who is to govern them. But the people can also choose to turn out their governors and elect new ones at the very next election. Third, our system is founded on the notion of equal opportunity. The doors are open to individual enterprise and achievement. Fourth, our economic system is based on private property. Although the government plays an important role in the economy, our system remains a capitalistic one in which decisions are made by many different individuals and groups operating in a market situation. Finally, we are a diverse nation, operating as a *pluralist* society. People do not have to conform to a single political line. Indeed, it is understood that people should organize into groups that represent their interests in order to compete in the political arena. It is also understood that if people do not want to join any group, they are not obligated to do so.

Just as the revolution helped to shape the American ideology, so too did the abundance of free land on the American frontier help to shape the American character. On the frontier the new Americans were physically isolated from Europe. Thrown upon their own resources, they soon became resourceful. Placed in an independent position, they became independent. Forced to think mainly about the problem of survival, they became hard-headed and materialistic. The frontier helped to create a democratic sense of every person's worth. European titles meant little there, where all people were just as good as their labors made them. The fact that land was both abundant and relatively cheap meant that social divisions based on unequal land ownership could not develop. Americans became an optimistic people because they could always pull up stakes and begin life anew somewhere else.

Americans as a nation were also shaped by the simple historical fact that they had never experienced a feudal age. As Alexis de Tocqueville wrote, Americans "arrived at a stage of democracy without having to endure a democratic revolution, and they are born equal instead of becoming so." Europe's revolutions were fought with an intensity that few Americans understood. European revolutions were fought to bring about sweeping changes in the social structure of its society. The American Revolution, on the other hand, was fought to produce a limited, if important, political change. Although some social and economic changes were linked to this political change, they were subordinate. The American revolutionary tradition is thus a limited one in the European sense of the term. That America has had no feudal background to overcome has meant that Americans have not developed the class antagonisms found in European society nor the class lines once revered in Asian society. Americans, consequently, find European political movements that touch upon class conflicts difficult to understand.

America's foreign policy has been strongly influenced by its ideological beliefs. In principle, if not always in practice, the United States has been concerned with creating a world environment in which other peoples can enjoy the same basic freedoms that Americans have.

None of these concerns apply to Soviet foreign policy. The behavior of the Soviet Union in world affairs has been shaped by a combination of traditional Russian state goals and the revolutionary international ideology of Marxism-Leninism. The uneasy coexistence of these two strains has made it particularly difficult for Western statesmen to deal with the Soviet Union. Westerners have always had trouble understanding the goals and motives of Soviet leaders. Winston Churchill once described the Soviet Union as a "riddle wrapped in a mystery inside of an enigma." Russia, over the centuries, has never been sure whether it belongs to the East (Asia) or to the West (Europe). The sense of duality generated by the pull of two different cultures has tended to make Russian policies even more confusing.

Before 1917 Russia was a great feudal empire ruled by Romanov czars (or emperors). A small nobility was supported by a mass of agricultural serfs. Russia had virtually no middle class and no tradition of democratic liberties. Russia's foreign policy before the revolution was governed by geography and by the vast size of the Russian empire. Almost completely landlocked, Russia has always tended to try to expand in all directions. The czars always experienced difficulties in trying to rule a huge territory, one that stretched from the Baltic and Black seas to the Pacific Ocean and that contained over one hundred different nationalities.

The Czarist rule was overturned by a democratic revolution in February 1917. The Bolsheviks (Communists) carried out their own revolution in October 1917. The old Russian empire became the Union of Soviet Socialist Republics. Compared to Western Europe, the new Soviet state was a backward nation. (For instance, it did not industrialize until the 1930's.) Having been isolated from other nations until World War II, Russia had little experience in conducting foreign policy. This inexperience made relations with the West much more difficult after World War II.

An important aim of Soviet foreign policy was to maintain the territorial ambitions of the old Czarist regime. But that policy was also shaped by a practical ideology, Marxism-Leninism. Karl Marx was a German who as an exile developed his theories in the library of London's British Museum. He was a nineteenth-century radical who criticized the capitalist system as unjust. He was not just a reformer; he was a revolutionary. Marx wanted a revolution that would sweep away the entire capitalistic social order.

Marx claimed that his kind of socialism was scientific. He believed that he had discovered objective historical laws — much like the laws in the natural sciences — which determined the course of events, irrespective of what people did. One of these laws was that the struggle between the social classes was the most important development in human history. Marx called his philosophy "dialectical materialism." According to this theory, the dominant interest of all people is in material gain; peoples' ideas are only a reflection of their economic self-interest. Their efforts to exploit their material surroundings generate a constant struggle between various social forces. According to Marx's schema, revolution was inevitable because the capitalists would bring about their own destruction by creating a *proletariat*—an industrial working class—who would eventually seize control of society from the middle class, who had earlier seized it from landholding nobles.

Marx offered a vision of a perfect socialist society that was idealistic and humanitarian—a society in which the goal would be "from each according to his ability, to each according to his need." But he did not say how people were to organize such a socialist state. Even as a future dream, Marx's ideas were vague. He was mainly concerned with criticizing capitalism. His failure to say very much about how the future socialist state should be organized posed serious problems for his followers. Marx saw himself as a prophet. Instead he was looked upon as a dreamer. The society that his followers created in Russia proved to be very different from even his vague dreams.

Vladimir Ilyich Lenin was a dedicated Russian revolutionary who, after spending most of his life in exile, applied Marx's writings to the Russian situation. Marx may have been the theorist of the Russian Revolution, but Lenin was its architect. Lenin was a superb tactician, who realized that in order to achieve his primary goal—the overthrow of the Czar—the writings of Marx would have to be adapted to Russia, for no large-scale capitalism had ever been practiced there.

Lenin added new chapters to the theories of Marx. He emphasized the importance of a revolutionary party (it became the highly disciplined Communist Party), which would make the revolution and control the new socialist state. Marx had predicted the withering away of the state after the revolution. This proved to be a fantasy. For Lenin believed the state would be necessary to direct society after the revolution. Lenin also developed the theory of the *revolutionary dictatorship of the proletariat*. This meant that the Communist Party—supposedly the "vanguard of the working class"—would speak in the name of all the Soviet peoples. Lenin's theories were thus well-suited to the seizure of power in a country that was largely backward, and that had only a tiny industrial class. In practice, Leninism meant that the state would control all activities in the Soviet Union since it owned all the property. But in the Leninist schema, the real power to run the state was to be concentrated in the hands of the relatively small Communist Party. Since no other group existed that could challenge the party's total monopoly over real power, elections would be mere window dressing.

When the Bolsheviks took power in 1917, it was a political revolution in that one government was overthrown and another came to power. Lenin died in 1924. His successor was Joseph Stalin. Stalin carried out a real social revolution in the late 1920's and 1930's. Private farming was abolished and replaced by agricultural collectives. All branches of the economy were nationalized — that is, taken over by the state. A system of rigid economic planning by party officials was established to achieve the industrialization of the country. Westerners might have been impressed by the speed and scale of the Soviet Union's industrialization. But they were appalled at some of Stalin's policies. He was as brutal a dictator as had ever lived. He created an elaborate network of security police, which was used to purge and kill off his political opponents during the "Great Terror" of the 1930's. Any freedom of expression that might have existed disappeared completely. Diversity of opinion was not tolerated. Stalin hardly stopped at these repressions. During the 1930's, millions of farmers who had resisted the collectivization of their farms were forced off their land and left to starve to death. Many more millions of Soviet citizens were arbitrarily arrested and sentenced to prison camps, where they perished. A casual conversation with a foreigner was often enough to warrant a death sentence.

Marx had virtually nothing to say about foreign policy. He assumed that there would be no national states in a socialist world, so there would be no need for a foreign policy. Lenin also paid scant attention to foreign affairs. Leon Trotsky, the first commissar for foreign affairs, saw his job as one in which he would only "issue a few revolutionary proclamations and shut up shop." However, there were no successful revolutions anywhere else in the first years after the Bolshevik Revolution, and Russia had to begin to interact with nonsocialist states. Eventually the Soviet Union realized that it had to function within the international system. It began to act more like a traditional power than a revolutionary one. That is, it shifted from promoting a world revolution to furthering the interests of Russia. By the time Russia came into large-scale contact with the United States after World War II, it seemed reconciled to functioning within an international system that was dominated by capitalists. Yet, it was not like other states. The Soviet Union was still a state founded on Marxist-Leninism, and it—at least in doctrine—remained dedicated to world revolution. The real question was to what extent the Soviets continued to believe that world revolution was possible.

*　　*　　*

The rift between the United States and the Soviet Union widened in September 1945, when the Council of Foreign Ministers met in London. No longer did the need for wartime unity obscure the fact that the Soviet Union was determined to carve out its own sphere in Eastern Europe. Most Americans opposed any sphere-of-influence arrangements. When he visited Moscow in October 1944, Churchill, representing a country experienced in power politics, had sought to make a deal, outlining British and Russian spheres in the Balkans:

> The moment was apt for business, so I said, "Let us settle about our affairs in the Balkans. Your armies are in Roumania and Bulgaria. We have interests, missions, and agents there. Don't let us get at cross-purposes in small ways. So far as Britain and Russia are concerned, how would it do for you to have ninety per cent predominance in Roumania, for us to have ninety per cent of the say in Greece, and go fifty-fifty about Yugoslavia?" While this was being translated, I wrote out on a half sheet of paper (these figures). . . .
>
> I pushed this across to Stalin who had by then heard the translation. There was a slight pause. Then he took his blue pencil and made a large tick upon it and passed it back to us. It was all settled in no more time than it takes to set down. . . .
>
> After this there was a long silence. The pencilled paper lay in the center of the table. At length I said, "Might it not be thought rather cynical if it seemed we had disposed of these issues, so fateful to millions of people, in such an off-hand manner? Let us burn the paper." "No, you keep it," said Stalin.

Initially, Russia seemed willing to restrict itself to exerting influence, at least in some countries. In Hungary, for instance, there was a semblance of democratic procedures, including a government led by a non-Communist peasants' party. In other countries, such as Bulgaria and Rumania, the Soviets interpreted influence to mean ruthless domination and excluded all non-Communists from a share of power. Stalin feared that free elections would result in anti-Soviet victories; he insisted on maintaining "friendly" regimes. Westerners, perhaps ignoring the lack of any democratic tradition in some of these states and their tradition of authoritarianism, were nevertheless appalled by the brutal exercise of Soviet power in its sphere.

The "Polish Question" had become the "Eastern European Question," and it was over the future of this region that the Cold War really began. The Soviet Union, represented by the dour Molotov (known as "Old Stoneface"), continued to reject Western protests at the London Conference. There seemed little question that the Russians were aiming to turn the recently liberated countries of Eastern Europe into dependent states. As Western opposition became more open, arguments broke out over technicalities of the conference itself, and it soon ended in mutual recriminations.

Secretary of State James Byrnes, who had made his reputation as a great compromiser when he had been the Senate Majority Leader, tried again to reach an understanding with the Soviets. In December he flew to Moscow and met personally with Stalin. He did succeed in making some important agreements and in easing the mounting mutual distrust. Others in the administration, recalling the Munich Crisis in 1938 when Britain and France had tried unsuccessfully to "appease" Hitler, now accused Byrnes of appeasement, of selling out vital American interests. This "get-tough-with-Russia" group, headed by Admiral William Leahy, won Truman over to its position. The President made clear that he opposed Byrnes's recent negotiations and reminded the Secretary that he, Truman, was still the boss.

The Republican Congressional leadership now demanded a tough policy, and the Republican foreign-policy spokesman John Foster Dulles warned the nation that its principles and ideals were soon to be bested by a Soviet challenge. Domestic party politics clouded the issue, as the Republicans found that they could gain the support of certain Democratic groups of voters by protesting Roosevelt's compromises on Poland and elsewhere in Eastern Europe. But the appeals for Soviet restraint, coming from both parties, fell on deaf ears, for Stalin measured power in terms of the number of divisions a nation could put into the field. One anecdote, perhaps apocryphal, sums up his viewpoint. He countered a reference to the moral power of the Papcy with the cynical query, "And how many [military] divisions does the Pope have?"

At the beginning of 1946, the lines on both sides began to harden noticeably. Since Roosevelt's two other postwar policemen, Great Britain and China, were too weak to influence policy, the world was polarizing between the United States and the Soviet Union. Great Britain, bled by the costs of war and plagued by economic decline, was becoming more dependent economically on the United States. China was embroiled in a civil war; it appeared that the emerging world-wide conflict was being acted out in miniature there. The two major powers became increasingly hostile. The Russians thought that the United States was trying to use nuclear blackmail to force them out of the security belt, which Soviet blood and arms had won in Eastern Europe. The Russians had demobilized 70 percent of their troops, a secret kept from the West; hence, they were in no position to make any real efforts to reach beyond the immediate border countries. In 1946, twenty-five million Russians were still homeless; devastation was everywhere. When drought was added to famine, tens of thousands of people died of starvation. Conditions were so bad that starving people in some regions resorted to cannibalism. Stalin was acting tough, but he was bluffing, in part, in his relations with the West.

The one area in which he did not bluff was Eastern Europe. The Russians used the Red Army, secret police, arbitrary arrest, intimidation, assassination, faked purge trials, and one-sided trade deals to win total control over Eastern Europe. The vivid memories of "Stalinization" affected American-Soviet relations for the next quarter century. Many Western policymakers came to fear that Eastern Europe was only the first step in a Russian effort to conquer the world, not so much through the Red Army but through subversion by local Communist parties. This view was forcefully stated by historian-diplomat George Kennan, the number-two man in the United States embasssy in Moscow, in an 8,000-word telegram that he sent to Washington in February 1946. The State Department distributed hundreds of copies to all high-ranking officials. This long telegram became required reading, the bible for policy-makers:

> World communism is like a malignant parasite which feeds on diseased tissue. . . . [W]e have a political force committed fanatically to the belief that with the United States, there can be no permanent *modus vivendi,* that it is desirable and necessary that the internal harmony of our society be disrupted, our tradi-tional way of life destroyed, the international authority of our state be broken, if Soviet power is to be secure. This political force has complete power of disposition over . . . one of the world's greatest peoples . . . deep and powerful currents of Rus-sian nationalism. In addition, it has an elaborate and far-flung apparatus for exertion of its influence over other countries. . . . In foreign countries, Communists will, as a rule, work toward destruction of all forms of personal independence — economic, political, or moral.

A few weeks later, Winston Churchill delivered his famous "Iron Curtain" speech at Westminster College in Fulton, Mis-souri. Although Churchill's party had been defeated in a gen-eral election six months before and he was now a private citi-zen, the British government still continued to follow his policies. The new Foreign Minister, Ernest Bevin, was a social democrat who had fought Communists in the trade union movement and viewed communism with horror as a be-trayal of the workers from the left. Now at Fulton, Churchill declared:

> A shadow has fallen upon the scenes so lately lighted by the Allied victory. Nobody knows what Soviet Russia and its Communist international organization intends to do in the im-mediate future, or what are the limits, if any, to their expansive and proselytizing tendencies. . . .
>
> From Stettin in the Baltic to Trieste in the Adriatic, an iron curtain has descended across the continent. Behind that line lies all the capitals of the ancient states of Central and Eastern Europe. . . . [A]ll are subject in one way or another not only to Soviet influence but to a very high and increasing measure of control from Moscow. . . .

In front of the iron curtain which lies across Europe are other causes for anxiety. . . . The future of Italy lies in the balance. . . . [I]n a great number of countries, far from the Russian frontiers and throughout the world, Communist fifth columns [supporters of the enemy within a nation] are established and work in complete unity and absolute obedience to the directions they receive from the Communist center. The Communist parties or fifth columns constitute a growing challenge and peril to Christian civilization. . . .

The phrase "iron curtain" was picked up immediately. Public reaction was mixed. Some thought the speech revealed an overdue truth. Others criticized Churchill's call for an Anglo-American military alliance. While President Truman, who had invited Churchill to Missouri, privately agreed with the thrust of the speech, he publicly took no responsibility. Stalin, enraged by the idea of an Anglo-American alliance, called the speech "a dangerous act . . . a call for war on the Soviet Union." He said that Churchill was advocating an "English race theory," which was leading some people "to the conclusion that the English-speaking nations, as the only superior nations, should rule over the rest of the nations of the world. . . . Possibly in some quarters an inclination is felt to forget about these colossal sacrifices of the Soviet people. . . . But the Soviet Union cannot forget about them. And so what can there be surprising about the fact that the Soviet Union, anxious for its future safety, is trying to see to it that governments loyal in their attitude to the Soviet Union should exist in these countries?"

There was evidence enough in the drumbeat of events through the rest of the year that a cold war was taking shape. Russia was using heavy pressure, including military threats, to extend its inflence over northern Iran and also to win oil concessions that matched those already won by Western companies. The issue went to the United Nations, where the United States, fearing that this aggressive step was only Russia's first move outside Eastern Europe, forced Russia to back down in a significant public defeat.

In the United Nations, the United States had also introduced a proposal for the control of atomic energy. It was named the Baruch Plan after its main negotiator, elder statesman Bernard Baruch. In introducing the plan at the United Nations, Baruch called the control of atomic energy "a race between the quick and the dead." The tedious debate in the United Nations, however, became a race between the bored and the slow. On the one side, the United States refused to relinquish control over its atomic secrets without adequate safeguards, including knowledge of what was happening inside Russia. On the other side, Stalin would never allow outside experts to wander freely through the Soviet Union. Russia's rejection of the Baruch Plan gave United States leaders further proof that George Kennan was right after all. Roosevelt's old dream for postwar cooperation could not work.

Germany was one area where cooperation had been working. Well into 1946, General Lucius Clay, the head of the American occupation, felt that relations with his Russian colleagues were going well on the Control Commission. It was inevitable, however, that the winds of this new storm would soon blow across Germany, which lay like a no-man's land between East and West. Neither the United States nor the Soviet Union could allow this damaged but still valuable prize, with its great industrial capacity, to be claimed by the other power. Russia still feared a revived Germany. Western leaders, already concerned about the failure of Western Europe to recover economically, concluded that the recovery of Germany — or at least the three-quarters they controlled — was essential to Europe's economic health. But they did not want to pour in aid from one side, only to have the Russians drain it off as reparations from the other side. And so in Germany, cooperation broke down, leaving the country divided in two. Nevertheless, Secretary of State Byrnes finally succeeded in negotiating peace treaties with the former German satellite states, and there was some hope that progress could be made on a German treaty.

A potentially more serious crisis developed in the summer of 1946 when the Russians began to apply heavy pressure on Turkey to win joint control of the Dardanelles strait. Stalin, like the czars before the revolution, had coveted warm-water ports that would not freeze over during the long Russian winter. The Russian ports on the Black Sea would be just that, so long as the Dardanelles was not closed to their ships. Moreover, Turkey's stock was not high because it had sat out the war as a neutral. When the Russians demanded joint control of the strait in August, the United States regarded it as a Soviet effort to catpaw into the Mediterranean. Truman would not allow it. "We might as well find out now, as in five or ten years, whether the Russians [are] bent on world conquests," he told his advisers. He informed the Russians that the United States would not agree to their proposal and would oppose them even if "it might lead to armed conflict." The crisis passed, as the Russians backed down, but events were happening fast.

In the winter of 1946–47, George Kennan was engaged in writing an article called "The Sources of Soviet Conduct," a sequel to his long 8,000-word telegram. When the article was finally published in *Foreign Affairs,* the author was listed as "Mr. X." Kennan had become chairman of the State Department's Policy Planning Council, and it was considered inappropriate for his name to be linked publicly with the article. Nevertheless, the identity of Mr. X soon became known, and the article created a sensation. It is often described as the most important magazine article ever published in America. Kennan summarized the attitudes toward the Soviet Union that had developed in government circles. He outlined the so-called "Containment Doctrine," which would guide American foreign policy throughout the entire Cold War until the very late 1960's. Kennan wrote that the Western world had to find "the strength and resourcefulness to contain Soviet policy":

> The main element of any United States policy toward the Soviet Union must be that of a long-term, patient but firm and vigilant containment of Russian expansive tendencies. . . . [I]t is a *sine qua non* of successful dealing with Russia that the foreign government in question should remain at all times cool and collected. . . . [T]he Soviet pressure against the free institutions of the Western world is something that can be contained by the adroit and vigilant application of counterforce at a series of constantly shifting geographical and political points, corresponding to the shifts and maneuvers of Soviet policy, but which cannot be charmed or talked out of existence. The Russians look forward to a duel of infinite duration, and they see that already they have scored great successes.

Political commentator Walter Lippmann challenged Kennan's thesis:

> Mr. X has reached the conclusion that all we can do is to "contain" Russia until Russia changes, ceases to be our rival, and becomes our partner. The conclusion is, it seems to me, quite unwarranted. The history of diplomacy is the history of relations among rival powers, which did not enjoy political intimacy, and did not respond to appeals to common purposes. Nevertheless, there have been settlements. For a diplomat to think the rival and unfriendly powers cannot be brought to a settlement is to forget what diplomacy is about. There would be little for diplomats to do if the world consisted of partners, enjoying political intimacy, and responding to common appeals.

Lippmann was one of the few critics of the Containment Doctrine, for it had been embraced by many Americans and most policymakers. By the end of 1947, doors had been shut, negotiations over Germany had broken down, and the period some call the High Cold War had begun. International politics had become bipolar, characterized by a division into two hostile blocks. The Containment Doctrine had been shaped into policy at the beginning of 1947, in response to Communist pressure on Turkey and Greece.

Greece had been occupied by the Germans during World War II. The upheaval of war had broken its old social order, and even before World War II had ended, civil war had broken out there. At first, a temporary truce was made between a right-wing government and the National Liberation Front (EAM), which contained both Communist and non-Communist elements. But, as with the Cold War, the situation in Greece polarized. Revenge became a way of life. The truce broke down, and civil war was renewed in full fury. Much of the aid to EAM came from Yugoslavia, the most independent of Russian control of the new Communist states in Eastern Europe. However, England and America became convinced that the real source of aid was Moscow. But whatever the source, Greece could not be allowed to go Communist. If that happened, Britain's imperial lifelines to India would be threatened. The security of the Mideastern oil pool would also be endangered.

In late February a British diplomat informed the U.S.

State Department that Great Britain, which had until then included Greece in its sphere of influence (since the 1944 Churchill-Stalin agreement), could no longer provide economic aid to that ravaged country. United States leaders swung into action, and within weeks, economic and military aid programs were devised for Greece. Acting Secretary of State Dean Acheson presented to a group of Congressmen the picture of what American leaders feared would happen if EAM won in Greece: The Russians would control Greece. "Turkey would sooner or later succumb . . . and then Iran." The Russians would soon control the entire eastern Mediterranean and the Near East and then — like dominoes — Asia and Africa would fall. One Senator advised Truman to present the picture publicly in order "to scare the hell out of the American people." The message was delivered by Truman to Congress on March 12, 1947. No longer was the conflict muted; Truman now drew this Cold War in stark, global terms:

> Totalitarian regimes, imposed on free peoples, by direct or indirect aggression, undermine the foundations of international peace and hence the security of the United States. . . . At the present moment in world history, nearly every nation must choose between alternative ways of life. . . . One way of life is based upon the will of the majority and is distinguished by free institutions. . . . The second way of life is based upon the will of a minority forcibly imposed upon the majority. It relies upon terror and oppression. . . . I believe that we must assist free peoples to work out their own destinies in their own ways.

And then the President quietly added what would be the creed of postwar American foreign policy. Though intervention was traditionally distasteful, the United States no longer had a choice: "Great responsibilities have been placed upon us by the swift movement of events. . . . If we falter in our leadership, we may endanger the peace of the world."

The Truman Doctrine gave body to the Containment Doctrine. It ended the civil war in Greece and prevented a Communist-led EAM victory. It signaled that the United States would take an active role in world affairs. Yet even Kennan criticized it as too ideological, too sweeping in its commitments.

Western Europe offered the ground for developing a more

comprehensive program. The situation there was "steadily deteriorating," one official wrote in 1947. "One political crisis after another merely denotes the existence of grave economic distress. Millions of people in the cities are slowly starving." Virtually all American leaders shared this view. Evidence of economic distress was everywhere. The Germans, defeated, inert, lived in rubble-strewn cities. In Italy, inflation had made American cigarettes a preferred currency. In France, transportation and food production were almost totally at a standstill. In England, half the coal mines were idle, and electricity was available in the cities for only three hours a day.

Meanwhile, on the European continent many industrialists and members of the upper classes had been discredited because they had collaborated with the Fascists and the Nazis. The Communist parties, on the other hand, had wide appeal. Communists had been effective and, in some cases, heroic leaders in the Resistance movements. In the midst of economic chaos, they also gained the support of many poor and desperate people. A Communist party, however, was not an ordinary party. Although outwardly it might express willingness to cooperate in coalition governments, once in power, judging by the models in Eastern Europe, it might well act as a Trojan Horse to seize police power and liquidate the opposition. American State Department officials agreed with George Kennan's fear that the Russians would draw tight "that invisible network" of national Communist parties and "bring the rest of Europe into the shadows which have already enveloped the East." American security was thus endangered not only by the economic collapse of Western Europe itself, which threatened America's economic well-being, but also by the possibility that the Russians might take advantage of the devastation and demoralization to seize control through subversion. Something dramatic had to be done—and immediately.

On June 5, 1947, the new Secretary of State General George C. Marshall delivered a short address at the Harvard University graduation ceremonies in which he unveiled the "Marshall Plan" to rescue Western Europe. He vividly described the dislocation and economic breakdown. Europe could not recover if it did not get loans and food for the next few years, principally from the United States:

It is logical that the United States should do whatever it is able to do to assist in the return of normal economic health in the world, without which there can be no political stability and no assured peace. Our policy is directed not against any country or doctrine but against hunger, poverty, desperation, and chaos. Its purpose should be the revival of a working economy in the world so as to permit the emergence of political and social conditions in which free institutions can exist.

The response to the plan in Europe was electric. "This is the turning point!" Ernest Bevin announced, leaping from bed upon hearing of Marshall's offer over the radio on the morning news. The plan placed emphasis on "self-help" and "mutual help." Even the Russians turned up at the preparatory conference. But, as with the Baruch proposals for atomic control a year before, the Russians would not participate in any program that provided for group planning and outside experts — despite their own desperate economic and social problems. They feared American economic domination. They shuddered at the economic power of their rival (at this time, the United States was producing half the world's entire industrial output). They did not want Westerners to see how weak economically Russia was. They also were afraid that they might lose control over the Eastern European nations. The Russians abruptly withdrew from the conference, forcing the Eastern European countries to follow suit. American officials, who had been holding their breaths, let out a sigh of relief. For they knew that the program would meet great difficulty in Congress if Soviet Russia was to be one of the recipients.

The Marshall Plan was an act of both generosity and self-interest. It not only restored Europe but also kept Western Europe firmly on America's side. It was so successful that, by 1949, the western part of the continent was well on the way to recovery. Moreover, the Marshall Plan launched the European "economic miracle," which culminated in the establishment of the powerful European Economic Community (EEC), or the Common Market, in 1957.

Despite its great success, the Marshall Plan divided Europe and brought about a bipolar world, composed of two hostile blocs. The Soviet Union had to respond to the great success of the Marshall Plan. On the other side of the iron curtain, Russia, through terror and purges, transformed its security bloc of client states into dependent satellites. In September 1947, at a secret meeting in Poland, the Soviet Union sought to bind the Communist countries together through a new propaganda organization called the Cominform. The leading Soviet ideologue, Andrei Zhdanov, as if responding to Mr. X, declared that the world was now divided into "two camps." In early 1948 the Communists brought down the parliamentary government of Czechoslovakia. This country had prided itself on being a bridge between East and West, as demonstrated by its own government in which non-Communist and Communist parties shared power in a coalition. The change in government put Czechoslovakia firmly in the Communist camp. When the Yugoslav Communist government of Marshall Tito refused to buckle under to Soviet demands, the Russians declared ideological warfare on that country. "I will shake my little finger and there will be no more Tito," Stalin is reported to have said. But, as Tito and his colleagues like to say, this was "a battle that Stalin lost." Tito, who had led the largest Resistance organization in Europe, had a genuinely popular following in Yugoslavia, and he was able to resist Stalin's efforts to undermine him. Yugoslavia remained independent and later led the efforts to create a "neutralist" bloc, outside both camps.

In 1948, when France, Great Britian, and the United States created a combined currency for their three zones in Germany, the Russians interpreted this action as a step toward the creation of a united Western Germany. The Russians responded by blockading West Berlin, stopping all road and rail traffic into that isolated city, 110 miles inside the Eastern zone, thus cutting off its food and fuel supplies. The United States, rather than cave in or risk all-out war, initiated the Berlin Airlift. For 324 days, American B-29's carried supplies — 13,000 tons a day — into the beleaguered city. At last, realizing the futility of the blockade, the Russians permitted ground transport again. The West continued with its plans to create a united Western Germany. Meanwhile, in 1949 the Western European states strengthened their allegiance to the United States that the Marshall Plan had generated by joining with the United States in a military alliance called the North Atlantic

Treaty Organization (NATO). For the first time since 1793, the United States was part of a permanent alliance. NATO was a logical step in the Containment Policy enunciated by Kennan and put into effect by the Truman Doctrine in 1947. The Russians responded a few years later with the Warsaw Pact, which formally linked the Eastern European countries to a Soviet military system.

One ingredient in the Cold War confrontation was absent. The Russians soon remedied that omission. On September 22, 1949, President Truman went on the radio with a simple announcement: the Soviet Union had successfully tested an atomic device. "This is now a different world," Senator Vandenberg said. It was. Europe was already divided; the world seemed poised permanently on the edge of war.

The Soviet development of the atomic bomb brought about an important change in the Cold War. Eventually both sides produced enough nuclear weapons to destroy human life on this planet, many times over. Thus, nuclear weapons introduced a new, if fragile, kind of stability, in which the balance of power was replaced by the balance of terror. The theory that explains this kind of stabilized relationship is called "deterrence." In practice, it means, for instance, that if the Soviets should ever decide to invade Western Europe, they know that the United States would immediately respond by launching nuclear weapons against the Soviet Union. So the Soviet Union is not likely to take any steps that might result in nuclear war. Similarly, the United States is not likely to take any steps to which the Soviet Union might reply with nuclear weapons. The nuclear umbrellas, which the United States and the Soviet Union hold above their heads, have served—however precariously—to prevent all-out war from breaking out between the two Superpowers. But the acceptance of nuclear deterrence has given rise to a new concept of warfare—limited war.

The Soviet explosion in 1949 shocked American leaders. They had not expected the Russians to develop an atomic bomb before the mid-1950's. Almost immediately, Truman gave the green light to develop the hydrogen bomb, a super weapon that would make the atomic bomb obsolete. On April 25, 1950, he approved a document prepared by the National

Security Council, called NSC-68, which Senator Henry Jackson has described as "the first comprehensive statement of a national strategy." Its basic assumption, as Secretary of State Dean Acheson recalled it, was "the conflicting aims and purposes of the two Superpowers: the priority given by the Soviet rulers to the Kremlin design, world domination; contrasted with the American aim, an environment in which free societies could exist and flourish." NSC-68 sought, in effect, to extend the Truman Doctrine and the Containment Policy to the entire world, with greater emphasis on military intervention. The price tag for NSC-68 was heavy; estimates indicated that the defense budget would have to be tripled, to between $45 and $50 billion a year. In April 1950, these plans were still secret and theoretical. It was unlikely that an economy-minded Congress would easily accept them. In June, however, the theory was put into practice and the price tag was accepted. The reason was that the Cold War had turned hot. A war of containment, a limited war, had begun, not in Europe, but halfway around the world, in Korea.

NO PEACE FOR ASIA

Harry Truman had just finished dinner in his old family home in Independence, Missouri, on June 24, 1950, when the telephone rang. Truman took the call in the library.

"Mr. President," said Secretary of State Dean Acheson, "I have very serious news. The North Koreans have invaded South Korea."

Truman's first inclination was to rush back immediately to Washington. Acheson suggested that he wait until the next day, when more information would be available. As it was, time would be short enough. For in a matter of days, Truman would face a fateful decision. It would be the culmination of the widespread crises that had developed in Asia after World War II.

That war had sounded the death knell for the old European colonial empires. Despite the defeat of Japan, there was no peace anywhere in Asia. The people of Asia were struggling for food to keep from starving, but they were also struggling for political rights. Everywhere guns continued to sound, as the social and political tensions aggravated by the war exploded from one end of the continent to the other. Nationalism was on the march, and the European countries fell back before it. The Japanese had ripped to shreds the symbolic authority of white Europeans; and no matter how hard Europeans tried, they could not reassert their authority. The once-great European powers, in their own wounded condition and worrying about coal and their own crops, could not even afford the effort. India, the jewel of the British empire, after decades of agitation, won its independence in 1947. It was partitioned into two countries, Hindu India and Moslem Pakistan. The vast archipelago of Indonesia became independent from the Netherlands in 1948.

Of all these battles, the one that mattered most in the late 1940's was not a colonial war but, rather, the civil war in China. The United States became deeply involved in the struggle over the future of that populous but disordered country. With little knowledge of China beyond that collected by a handful of diplomats, businessmen, and merchants—but with many romantic notions about this Asian giant—the United States found itself playing a role in China's domestic politics as soon as the war with Japan began in 1941. As our ally in the war, China received massive American aid—aid that went to the recognized government, to our ally Chiang Kai-shek.

China had been divided by revolution and civil war since 1927, when the National People's Party under Chiang took control of the government. Opposing Chiang was the Chinese Communist Party, led by Mao Tse-tung. Chiang might well have ruled effectively, if given the chance. His government from 1927 to 1937 was dictatorial; but it was more efficient than any other government that China had had in nearly a century. But the Generalissimo was unable to improve the condition of the peasants. The army, upon which his power rested, was often haughty and corrupt. No major reform program was carried out successfully, and the reforms that were achieved were nullified by the beginning of a full-scale war with Japan in 1937.

China was thoroughly disrupted by this new war. Fourteen million men were conscripted to defend the homeland against attack. Chinese Nationalists and, in particular, students and peasants felt that the major goal should be the defeat of Japan; internal dissension should be submerged during the war. When the United States entered the conflict four years later, it urged the same: Nationalist and Communist troops should fight together for the common cause of victory.

However, the Chinese Communists had two victories in mind, not one. They genuinely wished to see the defeat of Japan as an imperialist nation, and to this end cooperated with Chiang Kai-shek (and the United States). But they also were determined to emerge from the war with a considerably strengthened position, and this they did also. The Communists won a large following by preaching a "New China," promising material gains to the peasants — whose economic problems grew greater as the war progressed, thereby creating social conditions ripe for Communist expansion. The Communists aided the people among whom they were billeted by sharing their food supplies, while the Nationalist troops demanded the people's support as a right. And, most important to a nation already humiliated and prostrated by decades of war, the Communists claimed to be both modern and scientific.

Orthodox Marxist-Leninist doctrine held that the vanguard of the revolution must be the urban proletariat. But this clearly could not be the case in China, and so Mao began to put forward the then-heretical idea that the peasantry, not the proletariat, would be the spearhead of the Chinese revolution. In the late 1920's, he was already turning to a doctrine of guerrilla warfare, based on the support of the countryside. This was one of the many differences between Chinese and Russian communism that, despite a common Marxist allegiance, would always make the Soviet Union and China wary of each other and lead in later years to a bitter rivalry between them. Although Mao worked with the Russians when it suited both sides, he was his own man, and he created a distinctly Chinese form of communism.

The more obvious differences between the two Chinese leaders, Mao and Chiang, were never resolved, and the civil war was renewed even before the victory over Japan had been won. The United States tried to prevent this civil war by encouraging continued negotiations and by strengthening Chiang Kai-shek's government. Major efforts were made to clothe Chiang's government and army — which were virtually one and the same — with big-power status. Roosevelt insisted on including China in his "grand design" of Four Policemen for the world. His plan to have a strong, friendly ally in East Asia was partly realistic, and partly romantic as well, for Roosevelt was as attached to China as most Americans were. He delighted in recalling anecdotes about his merchant ancestors and their trade along the China coast in the early nineteenth century. To his British and Russian allies, who saw only a weak and corrupt Nationalist government, the idea of China as the fourth policemen seemed like a fantasy. Foreign Minister Anthony Eden told Roosevelt that China would probably have to go through a revolution after the war if it was to become a strong state; and he "did not much like the idea of the Chinese running up and down the Pacific." Nevertheless, the United States committed itself to the task of supporting Chiang's government.

At the end of World War II, Russian communism came into contact with Chinese communism. When the Russians occupied Manchuria, they supplied the Chinese Communists with captured Japanese weapons. Otherwise, Stalin did little to help Mao. The Chinese Communist leadership was disturbed by the Yalta agreement, which gave Russia a position in Manchuria like that once held by the old imperialist Western powers. "Soviet policy cannot be understood," the puzzled cadres in China were told. The leadership was even more incensed by the "correct" relations that Stalin maintained with Chiang and the Nationalists and by his general lack of interest in the Chinese Communists. Stalin was preoccupied with Europe. Moreover, he was apparently more interested in a weak, divided China, which would allow greater Russian influence in Asia, than in a strong Communist regime, which might (as indeed it has) draw upon Chinese nationalism and forcefully assert its independence of Moscow.

In December 1945, General George C. Marshall was sent to the wartime Chinese capital of Chungking to make a final attempt to stop the civil war and bring Chiang and Mao together. For the next year, he labored to unsnarl the China tangle, but the United States was by no means certain of what it wished to do. Toward the end of 1946, an American diplomat noted in his diary: "It is eerie to watch the growing confidence of the Generalissimo and his faith in his destiny." It was eerie because Chiang's Nationalist government had become corrupt, incompetent, and highly unpopular. Runaway inflation was adding to the woes of the Chinese people as a whole, most of whom seemed not to care which faction ruled so long as peace and stability were possible. Clearly, American self-interest dictated that the Communists should be stopped; but in the winter after the end of the world war, few in the West — least of all the American people — seemed prepared to fight a major war in Asia. The plain fact was that the situation in this Asian country of several hundred million people was beyond American control.

Chiang turned aside General Marshall's efforts to negotiate a settlement that would have given him the upper hand and, instead, decided on all-out war to defeat the Communists. But Chiang had chosen slow suicide, for his forces were not up to the battle. For the next three years, the civil war continued. The United States poured over $2 billion into Chiang's treasury, but internal economic collapse and ineffective leadership nullified most of the American aid. Despite an advantage in troop numbers and weapons, which at times was as high as five to one, the American-trained Nationalist forces were soundly defeated. In December 1949, they withdrew to Taiwan, to sit and hope that somehow, someday, they would be returned to power. In the same month, Mao flew to Moscow for three months of difficult and, for Mao, humiliating negotiations that helped to set the stage for the Sino-Soviet break a decade later.

Millions of Americans were critical of United States policy. They argued that China could have been "saved," if only the United States had intervened with more aid. The "loss" of China became a key issue in America's domestic electoral politics. Historian Stephen Ambrose has written:

> American success in 1917–18 (World War I) and 1941–45 contributed to the conceit that the United States could order the world. So did the awesome feeling of power that came with a monopoly of the atomic bomb, American productivity, and American position at the conclusion of World War II. There were racial connotations to the idea. Although most Americans were too sophisticated to talk about the "white man's burden," and the "little brown brothers," they still believed in white superiority. Many also held to the notion that the peoples of the Third World thought of Americans as being different because the United States had also come into being through a revolu-

tion. . . . Given all the power America had at her disposal, given American good will, and given the eagerness of peoples everywhere to follow the American example, how could it be that East Europe and China fell to the Communists?

Joseph McCarthy, the junior Senator from Wisconsin, had an answer. He charged that conscious neglect, even "traitorous actions" on the part of American diplomats, had led to China's loss. For otherwise, America could not have been "defeated." Declaring that the State Department was "thoroughly infested with Communists," McCarthy, in February 1950, waved a piece of paper no one ever actually read, and claimed that it held the names of 205 Communist sympathizers — later amended to 57 — in the State Department. George Kennan, whose own anti-Communist credentials cannot be questioned, has described how McCarthy's "witch hunt" destroyed the careers of honorable and capable public servants and had a "chilling" effect on political discourse:

> Everywhere, at that time, reputations were being attacked and damaged. Blacklists were being prepared. Innocent people were being removed from, or denied access to, employment for which they were qualified. Well-meaning citizens, normally humane and decent people, were busy purging libraries and screening textbooks for evidence of Communist influence. The records of faculty members were being combed over by zealots for signs of past heresy; and stern efforts were being exerted to see to it that the lecture platforms were denied to any who might be . . . dupes of the "Communist conspiracy." Thousands of good people were lending themselves in one way or another, as were large portions of the press, to this savage enthusiasm . . . mass hysteria.

With his rash charges, McCarthy divided the country into warring camps, inspiring terror in many public officials and ordinary citizens. When he finally overreached himself by taking on the United States Army and, by indirection, President Eisenhower, he was repudiated by the United States Senate and totally discredited in the public's eyes.

The truth of the matter was that China was never America's to "lose." The civil war in China resulted not from United States mistakes but from the wounds inflicted by Western and Japanese imperialism on a feudal Chinese society and by the dislocations suffered as China lurched into the modern industrial age. The forces of nationalism and communism spawned by these changes brought about the civil war. Can it even be imagined what it would have cost in dollars and in lives to have intervened in China! Even so, without a guarantee of victory, would Americans have wanted to pay those costs? Moreover, America's global strategy in a time of limited resources was, at this time, decidedly "Europe first." Europe was where the main struggle with the Soviet Union was centered.

The Communists had won ultimately because they were better organized and better motivated, and they were more successful in appealing to the poor masses. A State Department "white paper," which came out in 1949, perhaps too late to affect American public opinion, painted the sorry picture:

> The reasons for the failures of the Chinese Nationalist Government . . . do not stem from any inadequacy of American aid. Our military observers on the spot have reported that the Nationalist armies did not lose a single battle during the crucial year of 1948 through lack of arms or ammunition. The fact was that the decay which our observers had detected in Chungking early in the war had fatally sapped the powers of resistance of the Kuomintang. Its leaders had proved incapable of meeting the crisis confronting them, its troops had lost the will to fight, and its Government had lost popular support. The Communists, on the other hand, through a ruthless discipline and fanatical zeal, attempted to sell themselves as guardians and liberators of the people. The Nationalist armies did not have to be defeated; they disintegrated. . . .
>
> A realistic appraisal of conditions in China, past and present, leads to the conclusion that the only alternative open to the United States was full-scale intervention. . . . Such intervention would have required the expenditure of even greater sums than have been fruitlessly spent thus far, the command of Nationalist armies by American officers, and the probable participation of American armed forces — land, sea, and air — in the resulting war. Intervention of such a scope and magnitude would have been resented by the mass of the Chinese people, would have diametrically reversed our historic policy, and would have been condemned by the American people. . . .

The unfortunate but inescapable fact is that the ominous result of the civil war in China was beyond the control of the government of the United States. Nothing that this country did or could have done within the reasonable limits of its capabilities could have changed that result; nothing that was left undone by this country has contributed to it. It was the product of internal Chinese forces, forces which this country tried to influence but could not. A decision was arrived at within China, if only a decision by default.

By 1950, Chiang had retired to his "second China" on Taiwan to wait for his "restoration." Despite attacks in the United States from the loose coalition of some politicians and public-pressure groups called the China Lobby, which wanted "Chiang unleashed," the United States government was considering recognizing the new Communist government in China. There was no use in maintaining the fiction that Chiang's Taiwan was "China." Also, Chinese and Russian aspirations in East Asia had traditionally been opposed to each other. So it appeared that the United States could best serve its own interests by not provoking the Chinese Communists and by counting on Chinese nationalism to turn against Soviet imperialism. But the plans for establishing some kind of relations with the new Chinese government were delayed for many years – until President Nixon's visit in 1972 – by something else the United States had not counted on – the war in Korea.

The Korean War was a major turning point in the Cold War. It brought about the first direct military intervention in the United States in the name of the Containment Policy.

Called "The Hermit Kingdom," unknown to and isolated from much of the world, Korea had been a Japanese colony since 1910. At the end of World War II, when Russian and American troops entered Korea, the country was divided in two at the 38th parallel, with the Soviet Union occupying the north and the United States the south. In the immediate postwar years, Korea was virtually forgotten; the 38th parallel, meant to be a temporary division, became permanent as the Cold War intensified.

In 1947, when the United States asked the United Nations to sponsor a free election for uniting Korea, the Soviet Union refused to cooperate, fearing that a precedent would be set for uniting Germany. In the election, limited to South Korea, Syngman Rhee was victorious. The United States then provided Rhee with extensive aid, and the new republic became an American protégé. As the Communists tightened their control in North Korea, Rhee did the same in South Korea. While some Americans lauded Rhee as a heroic figure, others worried about his dictatorial ways, his use of secret police, and the economic decay in South Korea. Early in 1950, the United States government warned him to mend his ways.

After the Communist victory in China, the situation along the 38th parallel became very tense. Despite United States aid to South Korea, when Secretary of State Dean Acheson spoke to the National Press Club in January 1950 about America's defense commitment in the Far East, he implied that Korea was outside the American defense perimeter. The Korean Communists may well have interpreted his remarks as an admission that the United States would not intervene on that unstable peninsula. The leaders of both North and South Korea kept threatening to unify the country with military force. Armed incidents became common along the dividing line. Then, in the pre-dawn hours of June 25, 1950, the North Korean army moved in large force across the line. As the invasion began, the Cold War entered a new stage. South Korea seemed in danger of being overrun. On the map, a Communist Korea appeared to be a dagger pointed toward Japan..

Without hesitation, President Truman committed the forces of the United States to the defense of South Korea and to the United Nations. At 2 A.M. on June 25th, four and one-half hours after news of the invasion had been cabled to the State Department, the decision was made in Washington to request an emergency meeting of the United Nations Security Council. Just twelve hours later, the Security Council assembled. The Soviet delegate, who was boycotting the Security Council, was not present. By 6:00 P.M., the Council had passed a resolution charging North Korea with armed attack and ordering both sides to cease fire.

But who was to enforce this order? As the Security Council deliberated, President Truman, who was speeding toward Washington from his home in Independence, made a decision during the three-hour flight. World War II, he felt, had been caused by appeasement of aggressors; World War III might be prevented by resisting aggression. The United Nations had no troops with which to enforce its cease-fire order; so the United States, as a senior member of the United Nations, must shoulder the chief responsibility for enforcing an order which it had initiated. If "boldness be my friend," Truman would try boldness. At noon on June 27, Truman's pledge to provide American arms for the defense of South Korea was released.

Officially, the United States was not at war in Korea. Truman described American actions as an attempt to suppress a "bandit raid" and a "police action under the United Nations." Technically, this remained the situation, for there was no declaration of war and no negotiated treaty at the end. American troops were supported by British, Australian, New Zealand, French, Belgian, Dutch, Colombian, Ethiopian, Siamese, Greek, and Turkish forces. While the United States suffered 158,000 casualties (including 55,000 deaths), the South Korean troops sustained over a million. But the war seemed to Americans to be very much their war, for they virtually financed it; their generals led the United Nations command. American leaders rejected efforts by Great Britain and other allies to assume a role in policymaking.

At first, North Korean troops forced armies of the Republic of Korea and the United Nations forces into a pocket, around a bridgehead at the tip of the Korean peninsula. An American Dunkirk loomed. Then American sea and air power began to be felt; a blockade of North Korea and a steady flow of fresh troops from Japan stemmed the retreat, and the United Nations forces held on.

In a brilliantly executed maneuver, General Douglas MacArthur then turned the tide. Arrogant, aloof, and confident, MacArthur had become a legend in his lifetime—larger than life. During World War II, he had led American forces across the Pacific, back to the Philippines, and on to Tokyo Bay to receive the Japanese surrender. After the war, he had been governor of occupied Japan. With a studiously crushed campaign cap, a corncob pipe, dark glasses, and a "ramrod" bearing, he cut a commanding and daring figure.

MacArthur was determined to bypass the Communist strongholds and carry out an amphibious landing at the Communists' backs, at Inchon on the Yellow Sea, thirty miles above Seoul. Inchon was famed for its high tides, which meant that landings could only take place on three possible dates between September and November, and at only two times during the day on those dates. MacArthur is said to have heard this information and to have remarked, "The whole setup seems impossible. We'll do it."

At 6:00 A.M. on September 15, American marines carried out one of the most imaginative landings in their history. The North Korean troops fell back, disorganized, and within ten days Seoul was recaptured. The United Nations force swept all before it and reached the 38th parallel on September 30.

American troops had gone into action to regain South Korea, not to conquer North Korea; but the possibility of uniting Korea relatively easily was too great a temptation to reject. MacArthur was forced to pause, however, until a new resolution was passed by the United Nations on October 7, supporting the military unification of Korea. Then he drove across the border, and in the same month captured Pyongyang, the capital of North Korea. MacArthur remarked that the war might be over by Christmas.

Over by Christmas it nearly was, but not in the way that MacArthur had meant. As American troops pressed to within sight of the Yalu River, which divided Chinese Manchuria from North Korea, Mao Tse-tung acted. The Chinese had issued several warnings to the Americans to stay clear of their territory; they feared that this new advance might be the prelude to an invasion, perhaps to the use of an atomic bomb. In the first week of November, Chinese armies moved across the Yalu. Like a rubber band being snapped, the United Nations forces found themselves being repulsed with the same incredible speed with which they had moved forward. The retreat was disorganized and disastrous. In January, the United Nations forces abandoned Seoul, and once again the peninsula appeared to be on the verge of falling into Communist hands.

Then the war entered its fourth and final phase. It took weeks to overcome the sudden Chinese victories, but by February the surprise had been absorbed. Once again the United Nations forces inched forward. On March 14, they again entered Seoul. By spring, the army had moved into the mountains just north of the 38th parallel, and the front line was stabilized about where it stands today.

The next crisis created nearly as great a controversy in America as had the Communists' victory in China. It was brought about by President Truman's dismissal of General MacArthur for insubordination.

MacArthur had wanted to carry the war into China. He believed that the object of the war—to unify Korea—could be accomplished only if North Korea's chief defender was crippled. MacArthur wanted a naval blockade of the Chinese coast, the reinforcement of the United Nations command with Nationalist troops, a diversionary action by Chiang Kai-shek against the mainland, and the strategic bombing of Red China's industrial centers. He calculated that the Soviet Union would not come to Mao's defense. Not only would these tactics bring total victory in the Korean campaign but they would alter the entire balance of power in the Far East in America's favor.

Truman rejected these proposals. He felt that the Soviet Union would, in fact, come to the defense of its ally. An outright war with China would drain American resources, for China's manpower war far greater than America's. A full-scale war in Asia would divert American troops from Europe and expose our allies there to a Soviet attack. In any case, bombing Chinese centers would have little effect, Truman argued, for the Communists' main source for arms was the Soviet Union.

MacArthur was not convinced. Forgetting or unmindful of the fact that the United States has always cherished a tradition of government based on civilian supremacy, and that military figures are directly under the command of the President as commander-in-chief, he began to express his disagreement. In a letter made public in early April, he declared:

> It seems strangely difficult for some to realize that here in Asia is where Communist conspirators have elected to make their play for global conquest, and that we have joined the issue thus raised on the battlefield; that here we fight Europe's war with arms, while the diplomats there still fight it with words; that if we lose the war to communism in Asia, the fall of Europe is inevitable; win it and Europe most probably would avoid war and yet preserve freedom.... We must win. There is no substitute for victory.

Truman knew that the United States could expect to carry the war to China only against the opposition of its allies and of the United Nations. It would be a major war fought unilaterally by the United States. The present war was a stalemate; but a stalemate was preferred to an all-out war, possibly on two fronts, and without dependable Allied support. On April 11, President Truman announced that MacArthur had been relieved of his command. His place was taken by General Matthew B. Ridgway.

A nation-wide storm of protest broke over Truman's head. When he returned to the United States, MacArthur was hailed by many as a conquering hero. Some people saw this welcome as a prelude to a try for the Republican presidental nomination. (That designation, however, went to another acclaimed general, Dwight Eisenhower, who pledged to go to Korea to bring about peace.) Meanwhile, the Truman-MacArthur controversy raged on for several years in domestic politics, but the President had preserved the supremacy of civilian control. Eventually the controversy subsided. By the early 1960's, General MacArthur was warning his fellow Americans against becoming trapped in a land war on the mainland of Asia.

In July 1951, the Communist Chinese, now openly leading the North Koreans, agreed to meet with United Nations representatives to negotiate a cease-fire. Hopes that this would mean an early end to the war were short-lived, however, as the negotiations were protracted and periodically suspended. Not until May 1953 could even an exchange of sick and wounded prisoners of war be worked out. Finally, on July 27, 1953, an armistice was signed at Panmunjom, in an eleven-minute ceremony. Neither side had won, for the line separating North and South Korea now corresponded very closely to the 38th parallel. An inconclusive war returned Korea to an inconclusive peace, with the peninsula still divided into two hostile, armed countries.

Twice in the 1950's, confrontations developed over the tiny islands of Quemoy and Matsu in the Formosa Strait, which separated mainland China and Taiwan. Mao and Chiang regularly exchanged vows to "liberate" the other's realm. The Nationalist forces, in 1953, initiated bombing raids against the mainland coast. The following year, the Communists began to bombard Quemoy and Matsu, which were considered essential to the defense of Taiwan. The United States feared that this bombardment might be a prelude to a real effort to conquer Taiwan. In December 1954, Secretary of State John Foster Dulles negotiated a mutual security pact with Chiang, whereby the United States agreed to protect Taiwan; and Chiang, on his part, promised not to try to invade the mainland. Congress speeded through a resolution promising to defend the little islands of Quemoy and Matsu. The Seventh Fleet was ordered into the Formosa Strait, and the United States even considered a preventive air strike against the mainland. "I believe there is at least an even chance that the United States will have to go to war," Dulles told President Eisenhower. Faced with this show of determination, the Communists backed down. When Mao's forces again began to bombard Quemoy and Matsu in the late summer of 1958, President Eisenhower not only again ordered the Seventh Fleet into position, he also dispatched United States marines to Quemoy and Matsu, where they installed projectiles that could obviously fire atomic weapons. The Communists got the message, and the bombardment ceased.

STANDOFF IN EUROPE AND THE MIDDLE EAST

After the crises of the late 1940's, the continent of Europe settled down to an uneasy truce. Statesmen rattled their nuclear bombs, troops occasionally went on the alert, and signs of war were sometimes sighted. Underneath it all, both sides seemed to accept Europe's division into two spheres. Each side would do everything necessary to protect what it had but would think very carefully before meddling on the other side of the iron curtain.

Presiding over most of the 1950's was Dwight D. Eisenhower, who emerged from semiretirement as president of Columbia University to become President of the United States. He was a highly successful wartime leader in Europe, noted for his ability to win cooperation in situations where enmity had existed. He was personally charming, a figure people warmed to almost immediately. With an infectious grin and a rambling but sincere way of speaking, he was the model of the American hero — a Kansas farm boy who through hard work, a sense of duty, undeniable talent, and firm dedication to moral principles had been chosen to lead the people. As a candidate, he had promised, "I will go to Korea" to end the war there. Might he not also lead the American people out of the wastelands of the Cold War? So it was hoped. Remembering with some friendliness and nostalgia Russian-American cooperation during World War II, he was eager to improve relations with Russia.

America was not the only country with a new administration. Two months after Eisenhower became President, the aged Joseph Stalin was removed from power in the Soviet Union, not by ballots but by death. A mostly bloodless struggle for power ensued. The final victor was Nikita Khrushchev, a rotund, rambunctious former coal miner. Restless, impatient, colorful, he favored peasant proverbs and sometimes used language that made an interpreter's ears turn pink. Unlike the somber Stalin, who preferred to stay in the isolated security of the Kremlin, Khrushchev loved to junket around the world, grinning into news cameras. When an American diplomat said that he had seen a photograph of Khrushchev smiling atop an elephant in India, V. M. Molotov, foreign minister under Stalin and one of Khrushchev's rivals for power, snapped, "Yes, an elephant getting on an elephant." When Khrushchev finally visited the United States in 1959, he was bitterly disappointed that because of safety problems he was not allowed to visit Disneyland.

Khrushchev began the process of de-Stalinization, modifying some of the most repressive features of life in the Soviet Union and pulling back the iron curtain several inches. In 1956 he denounced Stalin's crimes in a secret speech (that soon became very public) and claimed that Stalin had been a cruel and ruthless tyrant. A major reason for the speech was purely political—to shore up Khrushchev's own position against his rivals—and he gingerly avoided any mention of his own previous role as a loyal lieutenant of Stalin. Khrushchev identified himself with the slogan of "peaceful coexistence," which meant a recognition that neither the Soviet Union nor the United States would disappear on its own and that, in a nuclear age, neither could attack the other without getting itself blown up in the resulting fray. Communism and capitalism, Khrushchev was saying, could exist next door to each other, as neighbors if not friends. The Russians had another reason for seeking improved relations with the West. Their Communist friends on the mainland of China were slowly becoming their rivals and competitors for leadership of the Communist world, and it was difficult to worry in two directions at once.

The Geneva Summit meeting, in 1955, held out some hopes that peaceful coexistence might be officially accepted by both sides. The Russians as well as the Americans agreed with Eisenhower's statement at this conference that either one of the two Superpowers could accidentally destroy the entire Northern Hemisphere. "War has failed," said the President. "The only way to save the world is through diplomacy." At Geneva, both sides seemed to accept the status quo in Europe. The successful negotiation of the Austrian Treaty in the same year, ending the occupation of Austria by the Western Alliance of World War II and setting that small country on a neutral course, also seemed a good omen.

Hostility ran deep, though, and the "Spirit of Geneva" did not long survive. The Russians, pressed by their more militant Chinese comrades and fearful of losing control over their Eastern European empire, could not afford to be too friendly to the West. Another reason was that Eisenhower left much of the execution of foreign policy to Secretary of State John Foster Dulles, an influential Wall Street lawyer, who came from a distinguished family of American diplomats. His diplomatic career had started at age nineteen when he attended the Hague Conference of 1907. He took a much harsher view towards the Soviet Union than did his chief. He doubted that relations could be improved. He regarded the Cold War as a fight to the finish between the forces of Good and Evil. He sought to employ religious thinking in the secular realm and sometimes seemed to suggest that God had joined NATO. He described as "immoral" the policy of neutralism, which the new state of India was following in order to avoid entanglement in the American-Russian rivalry. He also declared that mere containment was immoral, despite his own leading role in shaping bipartisan foreign policy under Truman. Instead, he spoke of "rolling back" communism, of "liberating" the peoples of Eastern Europe. He threatened "massive retaliation" against an aggressor and used the word "brinksmanship" to describe America's willingness to risk all-out war for specific foreign-policy purposes. Dulles' new "policy" turned out to be largely rhetoric, and the United States continued to pursue a policy of containment, but under other names.

One of the era's major changes was technological, with

the result that science and technology became a new battleground in the Cold War. The arms race spiraled during the 1950's; it was a race not merely for more weapons but for more sophisticated weapons. Major technological breakthroughs became common. Nuclear submarines, intercontinental ballistic missiles, and atomic rockets joined the arsenal of conventional weapons. The United States and the Soviet Union became different from all the other nations. They were not simply great powers; with their vast array of nuclear bombs, they were now Superpowers. Since weapons must be tested, both countries risked polluting the atmosphere with nuclear radiation as they repeatedly set off atomic explosions above ground. Neither side trusted the other enough to work out a meaningful nuclear-test ban.

The landmark in this new competition was really a "spacemark"—the Soviet Union's launching of a simple satellite into orbit around the earth in October 1957. The signals of this Sputnik (meaning "companion" in Russia), as heard in the United States, seemed to announce the end of American omnipotence. The nation was shocked into self-doubt. Something had gone wrong. How could the United States, which prided itself on being the most advanced country in the world, lose out in so crucial a matter to the Russians? Some Americans, recalling the race between the Soviet Union and the United States after World War II to sweep up German rocket experts, grimly joked: "Their German scientists are better than our German scientists." The Americans hurried to catch up. Our space program began to move at double time, and in January 1958, an American Explorer satellite went into orbit. One after another, American and Russian space vehicles penetrated the outer reaches of the earth's atmosphere and beyond. Both countries were in space to stay. The United States also sought to catch up by vastly increasing its investment in education, research, and development. (In the name of national security, money was poured into the educational system for everything from research grants for scientists to programs to teach algebra earlier in junior high schools and to introduce foreign-language instruction in elementary schools.)

United States and Russian leaders still kept their eyes firmly fixed on the map of Europe, for that continent remained the focus of concern. The one real sore spot was Germany. In May 1949, the part of Germany occupied by Great Britain, France, and the United States became the Federal Republic of Germany, with its capital at Bonn. Under Truman the United States supported and aided the rearming of this "new" country. To the expected outcries of the Russians were added the protests of the British and the French, but the United States had decided that German participation in the Western Alliance was necessary. Since the Alliance was led by the United States, the plan went through.

The Soviet Union created its own satellite state, the German Democratic Republic, known as East Germany. Although both the United States and Russia continued to call for the reunification of the two Germanys, in truth, neither side wanted to risk having a reunified Germany drift into an alliance with the other side or, even more unpredictably, having it become again a great power that would pursue an independent course.

The Russians began to have trouble with their new Eastern European empire. In June 1953, shortly after Stalin's death, workers took to the streets in East Germany to protest Communist policies and were put down by Russian troops. After Khrushchev's denunciation of Stalin in 1956, disturbances broke out in Poland; the Russians had to compromise by putting into power a more nationalist Communist regime, led by Wladyslaw Gomulka. A revolt that broke out in Hungary in October 1956 was brutally crushed by the Russians, whose tanks rumbled through Budapest, the capital of Hungary, firing at the "freedom fighters." The General Assembly of the United Nations condemned Soviet intervention in Hungary. Although the United States led the protest, it did not dare to intervene. Despite Dulles' rhetoric about "rollback" and "liberation," the United States could not try to fulfill those words when the opportunity arose for fear of touching off a general war that would end in nuclear devastation. The American reaction showed that the United States recognized that the Soviet Union had a sphere of influence in Eastern Europe that it would fight to the death to defend. The Russians equally recognized that they dare not venture into the richer, more heavily populated areas of Western Europe, without risking atomic retribution from the United States. So, tragic as it was for the Hungarians, the two Superpowers showed by their deeds and absence of deeds that they both would respect the status quo in Europe.

Late in 1958, Berlin flared into crisis again when Khrushchev tried to force the Western powers officially to recognize East Germany—in other words, to agree to a permanent division of Germany. He also wanted to break West Germany's ties with West Berlin. At first, Khrushchev virtually threatened war but almost immediately realized what a tight situation he was getting into. Soon after the crisis began, he said, "We would like to drink toasts again with wartime allies." He had the opportunity the next year, when he visited Eisenhower in the United States. The improved relations were now called "the spirit of Camp David," after the mountain-top retreat where Ike and Mr. K. talked privately for hours. The following year they met again for a summit meeting in Paris. On the very eve of the conference, however, Khrushchev announced that a Russian missile had shot down a high-altitude American U-2 plane and that the pilot had been captured. Initially, the United States claimed it was a weather plane, which had gotten lost. But Eisenhower soon admitted that it was a U.S. spy plane and took full responsibility. The conference broke up in mutual recriminations; the fragile spirit of Camp David was shattered. Some people argued that, according to diplomatic practice, Eisenhower should not have publicly accepted the blame, for by taking responsibility he made it impossible for Khrushchev to continue negotiating and still save face. The Americans were also faulted for not suspending flights during the summit.

Khrushchev's behavior, however, was far more puzzling. Why did he insist on making a public announcement? After all, spying by both sides was customary in the Cold War. Did he want to embarrass Eisenhower? Yet, he was looking forward to Eisenhower's return visit to the Soviet Union and had even secretly had a golf course built in the Crimea for the President's pleasure. Was his position being undermined by colleagues at home and by the Chinese comrades who said that he was not being militant enough? Was he trying for a quick victory? Or had he simply "flown off the handle" and, as was his wont, acted impulsively? The failure at Paris interrupted the growing dialogue between East and West.

During the Hungarian revolt of 1956, the United States had another reason for not reacting to it. About the same time, the question of who would control the Suez Canal erupted into a crisis that temporarily united the United States and the Soviet Union against Great Britain and France. This crisis was part of a growing Middle Eastern problem. Indeed, that problem involved a mass of competing forces—Arab nationalism, traditional Western influence versus Soviet efforts to gain influence and adherents, the old-line colonial powers of Britain and France versus the United States, which championed nationalism so long as it was moderate, anti-Communist, and friendly to the West.

An extra problem lay beneath the Middle Eastern sands—oil—64 percent of the world's known oil reserves, in fact. Without that oil, much of the Western world would grind to a stop. The problem had already bubbled to the surface in Iran, when Mohammed Mossadegh, a weepy, fiery politician who sometimes gave speeches in his pajamas, nationalized the Anglo-Iranian Oil Company. The case could easily be made that this British-owned company was exploiting Iran's oil, while paying very little back into the country. Iran was a poor, underdeveloped country, where five hundred out of every thousand babies died at birth. Mossadegh then began making overtures of friendship to the Soviet Union. Fearing that Iran might become another Russian satellite, the United States actively intervened in 1953. (The CIA organized domestic opposition and managed the goup that overthrew Mossadegh and returned the Shah to power.) Iran was returned to the Western camp, and the oil agreements were renegotiated to guarantee the Iranians a fairer share of the profits. A grateful Shah made sure that the American companies were put on an equal footing with the British, their old oil rivals in the Mideast.

Meanwhile, in July 1952, there had been a coup in Egypt that overthrew the monarchy. Two years later, Colonel Gamel Abdel Nasser, who had emerged as virtual dictator, pressed for reforms and declared himself neutral in the Cold War. He also became a spokesman for the rapidly emerging forces of Arab nationalism. He and the British negotiated a plan for ending British occupation of the strategically important Suez Canal Zone. On July 19, 1956, Secretary Dulles, irritated by

Nasser's neutralism, announced that the United States was withdrawing its offer to help Egypt build the Aswan High Dam, an important project to expand Egypt's irrigated agricultural land. Egypt now swung sharply leftward. Nasser desperately needed aid, and the Soviet Union promised to give it. A week later, Nasser nationalized the Suez Canal.

The Suez Canal had been Britain's lifeline of empire ever since the nineteenth century. It was of great military importance. It was also the channel through which sailed the tankers laden with "black gold," the Middle Eastern oil. The British Prime Minister, Anthony Eden, was determined to get the Canal back. On October 29, 1956, Israeli forces invaded Egypt, and the following day both Great Britain and France came to Israel's support, ostensibly to protect the Canal. Suez was the last stand of two old European colonial nations.

The United States, facing an acute dilemma, decided that it could not support what it considered to be "aggression," even if committed by its two closest allies. It voted with the Soviet Union on a Security Council resolution condemning Great Britain and France. Under heavy pressure from the United States and the United Nations, Great Britain and France finally gave in and agreed to a cease-fire on November 7. The Canal was restored to Egyptian hands, and the Soviet Union gained new followers in Africa and the Middle East. This episode was the beginning of Soviet influence in Egypt. The United States gained as well, winning new admiration and respect from both neutralists and anticolonialists for its evenhanded position. Egypt remained a cener of unrest in the Middle East as Nasser dreamed of a broader union of Arab states.

Arab nationalism continued to grow. In 1957 President Eisenhower received from Congress the power to use American military forces to stop Communist aggression in the Middle East. The policy, which became known as the Eisenhower Doctrine, was put into effect the next year when the President sent 14,000 American troops to Lebanon to keep peace in a crisis involving that country and neighboring Iraq. The crisis did not prove to be as severe as the United States government had thought. When the American troops hit the beaches, they were met not by hostile troops but by ice-cream vendors!

By the end of the 1950's, Europe had begun to regain its independent voice. Six countries — France, West Germany, Italy, Belgium, the Netherlands, Luxembourg — had taken steps in 1952 to begin unifying their industries and ending trade barriers. In 1957, with the Treaty of Rome, they formed the European Economic Community (EEC), or the Common Market, an economic union that matched the United States in output. With the prosperity that is necessary for stability assured, the creation of a united Europe seemed possible. The United States, mindful of how dangerous European divisions had been in the past, actively supported its Western European allies in this venture. The rebirth of Europe, giving rise to a "third force," helped lessen the bipolar confrontations that had been basic to the Cold War.

As President Eisenhower prepared to leave office in January 1961, he could take some comfort in the record of his administration. True, the Cold War was not over, and the "captive peoples" had not been liberated. Yet neither had the world ended in a nuclear war that had always seemed so close. The tensions between East and West had eased; the confrontations were less rigid. Both Superpowers recognized that each side had some vital interests that could not be challenged by the other side without threatening war. And general war, both sides believed, was not in anybody's interest.

Something else, however, disturbed the old warrior. President Washington, in taking leave of the country in his 1796 Farewell Address, had warned against "entangling alliances." Eisenhower, in his 1961 Farewell Address, warned against a different kind of entangling alliance — "the conjunction of an immense military establishment and a large arms industry" — the "military-industrial complex." The temporary institutions of World War II had become permanent; NSC-68 had come to life. And the President, whose own patriotism and military insight could not be questioned, was worried about this complex, "new in American experience," whose "total influence" was "felt in every city, every statehouse, every office of the federal government." Although he was not suggesting that any plots or coups or deliberate designs were involved, he did urge his countrymen to "guard against the acquisition of unwarranted influence, whether sought or unsought" by this complex. "The potential for the disastrous rise of misplaced power exists and will persist."

John F. Kennedy, Senator from Massachusetts, who had defeated Vice-President Nixon by the thinnest of margins, succeeded to the Presidency in 1961. Young, dynamic, handsome, vigorous, he seemed in so many ways a contrast to the grandfatherly Ike. Kennedy promised to get the country "moving again." He had often suggested in his campaign that the country had been sleeping while President Eisenhower fiddled on the golf course. (But he managed to keep his own fondness for, and skill at, golf top secret.) "The torch has been passed to a new generation," said Kennedy in his inaugural speech. While the generation was new, many of the policies were the same old ones. Upon taking office, Kennedy discovered that the "missile gap," which he had claimed during his campaign was in the Russians' favor, was actually in our favor. Nevertheless, ignoring Ike's warnings about the military-industrial complex, he went ahead with a further arms build-up. The Russians responded with their own, and the arms race went off on another upward spiral. Kennedy continued the same European policies. In June 1961, he had an unproductive meeting with Khrushchev in Vienna. Then another crisis flared up in Berlin. The Russians built a wall of barbed wire through the city and protected it with machine gun-bearing guards, in a successful effort to stop the flight of East Germans — 153,000 in the first eight months of 1961 alone, many of them young and talented — through the escape hatch at West Berlin. Once again, a crisis seemed to be moving the Superpowers to the edge of war, but the two powers backed away from that brink.

As time went on, contacts between Eastern and Western Europe increased. Life began to improve somewhat on the far side of the iron curtain. The insecurities diminished, as each Superpower realized that the other would not dare to do anything reckless in Europe. Slowly, the Cold War "glacier" receded from the continent of Europe. It could not be said that the Cold War was ending; the battle was simply shifting to other fields. The vacuums in Europe had been filled, but now there were new vacuums brought on by nationalism, the decline of the colonial powers, and the emergence of what was called the Third World.

CONFRONTATION
IN LATIN AMERICA

"In a week, we shall be dead." These were the words of the British philosopher Lord Russell on October 23, 1962. It was the week of the Cuban missile crisis; the eyes of people all over the world were glued to the steady movement of the clock's hands. If Russell had been proved right, there would be no one here to remember what happened. As it was, this crisis was the tensest moment of the Cold War, a very close call. The two Superpowers almost went over the brink. In a memorable phrase, Khrushchev would afterwards recall that it was a time "when the smell of burning hung in the air."

The missile crisis represented the expansion of the Cold War into the New World. The United States had traditionally pursued two policies in its attitude toward Latin America. One was that of the Good Neighbor, enunciated by Franklin Roosevelt in 1933. It meant an awareness that the Latin American countries were equal to the United States in their sovereignty. In this context the United States stood for democratic government, for progress, for economic development. The other policy was suggested by a comment of Secretary of War Henry Stimson in 1945: "It's not asking too much to have our little region over here which has never bothered anybody." This "little region" included all of the American continents, from Mexico to the southern tip of Chile, and also the Caribbean islands. Many Americans believed that our country, with its overwhelming political, economic, and military power, could and should preside over the destiny of the Americas, intervening at times to remove governments or to put new governments in power. The region was ours, both as a market and as a source of raw materials. The ultimate sanction for such an attitude was the Monroe Doctrine of 1823, issued to keep European influence out of Latin America.

For many of the peoples in Latin America, forced to live in shanty towns made out of cardboard and tin or in poor villages, the United States was not viewed as the "Good Neighbor" but rather as the "Colossus of the North." American companies carved out vast plantations to grow bananas and sugar and got large mining concessions to remove copper and oil. Much of their extensive profits went back to the United States, while the peoples of Latin America remained seemingly locked into a life of permanent underdevelopment. The national governments were, in most cases, either military dictatorships or "republics" that really represented only the small upper classes.

Further complicating the relations between the *Nord Americanos* and the *Latinos* was the question of race. Although the peoples of Latin America are the most mixed of any continent, racial stigmas are almost unknown. Yet, the Latin Americans feel that many citizens of the United States look down on them, especially if they have a dark skin. In such an environment, radicals who charged that the "little region" of Latin America was really an informal colony of the United States would win a wide hearing. Communism, especially, could make a strong appeal, for it not only opposed American policies and the native elites, it also claimed that it could deliver a better life to the poor.

In the 1950's, when the Russians began stepping up their propaganda efforts to win new converts to their side, the Cold War came to Latin America. The United States redefined the Monroe Doctrine so that it was no longer directed against the aging colonial powers of Europe but rather against communism, the new colonizer from the Old World. In 1954 John Foster Dulles said that the Monroe Doctrine now opposed "the domination or control of the political institutions of any American state by the international Communist movement." Making good on that pledge, the CIA sponsored a coup in Guatemala in the same year, which turned out a radical government that had nationalized the lands and railways of the United Fruit Company and had, more disturbingly, begun to seek and accept arms from the Communist bloc. The problem with such a restatement of the Monroe Doctrine was that it also seemed to set the United States against urgently needed reforms in Latin America. For instance, in Guatemala, 2 percent of the landowners controlled 60 percent of the land.

Nowhere was the dilemma of the two sides of the Monroe Doctrine more acute than in Cuba. Although United States intervention helped Cuba gain freedom from Spain in 1898, the independence that the United States then granted Cuba in 1902 was something of a fiction; the United States had insisted that Cuba write into its constitution the Platt Amendment, giving the United States a free hand for future intervention. And Cuba also leased Guantanamo Bay to the United States as a naval station. The power that the United States held over Cuba created a deep well of "Yankee phobia" among Cuban nationalists and intellectuals, even after the Platt Amendment was abrogated in 1934 as part of Roosevelt's Good Neighbor Policy. The year before, an army revolt had put Fulgencio Batista into power. This sergeant-turned-dictator, who ruled until 1958, built his power not only on the army, which was usual in Latin America, but also on organized labor. He even tolerated the Cuban Communist Party. For the peasants, he did little.

Cuba was not a poor country, by Latin American standards. It had a large middle class; over half the population was urban, and its per-capita income was nearly as large as Italy's. Yet there was widespread poverty. This poverty was linked to American influence, which many Cubans believed was keeping Cuba permanently underdeveloped. Almost as an economic corollary to the Platt Amendment, the United States had come to dominate the economic life of the country. By 1956, American companies owned 90 percent of Cuba's telephone and electric services, 50 percent of the railways, and dominated the sugar industry, which was responsible for 80 percent of its exports. In 1946, 70 percent of the land was held by 8 percent of the farms. The sugar industry offered only

64   THE COLD WAR

seasonal employment, which meant that 88 percent of the field and mill workers were employed only four months of the year. For the rest of the time, the landless plantation class lived in poverty, without running water, electricity, and often even without kerosene for light. (Cuba was wide open to another kind of American economic activity as well. In the 1950's, Mafia money began to flow into Cuba, taking control of much of the resort and tourist industries. Mafia exploitation of gambling, drugs, and prostitution became an especially unfortunate symbol of American influence.) Earl Smith, one of Eisenhower's ambassadors to Cuba, explained to Senators that the United States was "so overwhelmingly influential in Cuba that . . . the American Ambassador was the second most important man in Cuba; sometimes he was even more important than the [Cuban] President."

On July 26, 1953, a twenty-six year-old lawyer named Fidel Castro led an attack force of two hundred students on a Batista stronghold near Santiago. The attack failed, and Batista carried out gruesome reprisals. Castro and his brother Raul were jailed but secured their release two years later under a general amnesty. Fidel Castro went to Mexico, collected arms, money, and men — including an Argentine revolutionary named Ernesto "Che" Guevara — and in November 1956 made a landing on Cuba's shore. Again defeated, he escaped with a tiny band into the Sierra Maestra mountains. He now called his revolution the Twenty-Sixth of July (*26 Julio*) movement, after the date of his first battle.

Within two years, Castro was the victorious new prime minister of Cuba. It is not clear whether Castro was a Communist in the Soviet sense at the time, and by now even he may no longer remember. The revolution was in fact engineered largely by middle-class urban intellectuals, students, and professionals, who expected Castro to carry out basic reforms. Batista also helped to defeat himself; his habitual atrocities, sadistic and grim, finally disgusted even the army. The United States continued to give Batista aid until March 1958. Although the aid was not great, it was enough to link the United States with Batista in the minds of the revolutionaries.

On January 1, 1959, Batista fled to the United States, leaving Cuba to Castro, who pledged democracy, constitutional freedom, and land reforms. Within a few months, he was beginning his swing to the left. The leftward swing was supported by those closest to him, his brother Raul and "Che" Guevara. Soon his programs began to resemble those of Communist countries. For example, he called for collective farms instead of agricultural cooperatives.

Castro paid an unofficial visit to the United States in 1959. The bearded revolutionary, wearing green fatigues and puffing fine Havana cigars, was a puzzle to the Eisenhower administration. United States officials did not like him, but they did not know what to do about him. They were cautious and took an attitude of "let's wait and see."

By October 1960 the waiting seemed to be over. Some leading figures of the revolutionary movement and government, who were beginning to protest Communist influence, were imprisoned by Castro. In February 1960, Cuba and the Soviet Union signed a trade agreement; in June, American and British oil refineries in Cuba were expropriated. In July, the United States placed an embargo on imports of Cuban sugar, an almost overwhelming blow by the island's best customer for its one major crop. In the same month, arms from Communist Czechoslovakia were shipped to Cuba. If any doubts remained, Khrushchev, at last scenting a victory outside Russia's immediate sphere, announced that the Soviet Union would use rockets against any nation that attacked Cuba. In one of his very last acts as President, Eisenhower, on January 3, 1961, broke off diplomatic relations with Cuba.

John F. Kennedy, shortly after becoming President, launched the Alliance for Progress as a kind of Marshall Plan for Latin America and as a reassertion of the Good Neighbor policy. The United States would support economic development on a large scale, while Latin American countries would carry out political and social reforms in order to remove the inequities and poverty that communism exploited. The Alliance fell far short of its goals. It was not easy to pry the money out of Congress. The Latin American leaders were not willing to support the necessary reforms, which would have undercut their own wealth and power. Moreover, many Latin Americans were cynical about the program because they believed that the only reason the Americans had instituted it was their fear that Castroism would be exported. In other words, they thought the main motive for the program was containment.

Containment, however, was not enough for the United States. The very existence of the Castro regime seemed a threat to American interests in the hemisphere. Moreover, considerable domestic tension arose over the fact that a Communist state sat a mere ninety miles from United States territory. In the last months of the Eisenhower administration, the CIA had begun working out an invasion plan. Kennedy gave his approval of the venture, which was to be carried out by Cuban exiles, some of whom were disillusioned former members of the *26 Julio* movement.

The invasion carried out at the Bay of Pigs was a total failure. The fifteen hundred men who waded ashore on April 17, 1961, never got farther than the beach. No popular uprising met them; thus isolated, the men were either captured or killed. It was a stunning blow to the new President. Those who had planned the invasion had mistakenly assumed that the anti-Castro attitude of Cubans in Miami would be shared by the peasants in Cuba (to whom Castro was a hero). In addition, Kennedy, unwilling to take international risks, had kept overt United States military support, especially air cover, to a minimum.

Many influences had shaped Kennedy's decision to chose a "middle" course between all-out United States intervention and no intervention at all. He and his advisers believed that Castroism was a threat to the hemisphere. The Republicans and Southern Democrats went further, charging that Castroism was a specific threat to United States security itself. On the other hand, an all-out invasion would have made many new enemies for the United States; it would have, almost certainly, disrupted the Alliance for Progress, and perhaps would have resulted in a confrontation with the Russians.

On all sides, the results of this fiasco were bad for Kennedy: Cuba became an even more explosive issue in domestic politics. Castro acquired new sympathizers in the Western Hemisphere. Khrushchev's truculent attitude toward Kennedy at Vienna, in June 1961, had apparently resulted from the Russians' belief that incompetence lay behind the Bay of Pigs disaster. "There is an old saying that victory has a hundred fathers and defeat is an orphan," said Kennedy. Publicly he took responsibility. Privately he threw up his hands in exasperation with the CIA: "All my life I've known better than to depend on the experts. How could I have been so stupid, to let them go ahead?"

Castro now pulled out all stops on his march leftward. In December 1961 he declared that he was a Marxist-Leninist and would be "until the last day of my life." Three months later, he ominously declared: "The duty of every revolutionary is to make a revolution." This statement was more rhetoric than anything else on Castro's part; for, if not overthrown, he was increasingly contained — even isolated — by joint action of the Organization of American States. As Castro's problems mounted with this Latin American group, he had to find another market for Cuba's sugar; so he expanded trade with the Communist bloc. He also sought weapons from them.

In the middle of October 1962, United States high-altitude reconnaissance planes definitely confirmed that the Soviet Union was in the process of installing missiles in Cuba. Castro, on his part, wanted the guarantee of Soviet interest, represented by the missiles, to protect Cuba from another American intervention; the missiles would also make him more secure in his bellicosity. The Russians, in turn, wanted to protect their "investment" in Cuba, the newest member of the Communist bloc. They also were irritated by the presence of American missiles in Turkey. More important, Cuba offered a cheap way to gain some ground on the missile gap, which was so dramatically in America's favor. Finally, Khrushchev may have thought that missiles in Cuba would give him a trump card in forcing a deal on Berlin.

For the Americans, the presence of missiles, only a few minutes by air from cities like Washington, New Orleans, and Houston, was intolerable. It was a provocative and dangerous act by the Russians; it threw all of America's strategic planning into disarray. It also might have set off an explosion in the already overheated reaction of American public opinion to the Cuban problem.

At the height of the crisis that followed, John Kennedy had said to his brother Robert, "Really, there was no other choice. If they get this mean on this one, in our part of the world, what will they do on the next?" His brother agreed, adding, "If you hadn't acted, you would have been impeached." After a moment's thought, the President replied, "That's what I think — I would have been impeached."

What to do? Kennedy had assembled a top-level group, an Executive Committee (Ex-Comm) composed of top officials and elder statesmen, to advise him through the crisis. They concluded that an invasion or air strikes might lead to all-out war. No action, also, threatened serious consequences. The solution lay in a "quarantine of Cuba," that is, a naval blockade of all ships carrying offensive weapons to the island. This course had much to recommend it; there would be a day or two between the announcement of the decision to blockade and the first contact with a vessel, thus giving Khrushchev time to see that the United States meant to stand firm.

On the evening of October 22, a grim-faced Kennedy went on television to announce that the United States faced its most serious Cold War challenge in a decade. In his speech he warned the Soviet Union that any attack launched from Cuba against any nation in the Western Hemisphere would bring instant and full-scale nuclear retaliation, directly against the Soviet Union. The Air Force was placed on the alert; a fleet of B-52 bombers, already in the air, was prepared to strike. Every ship headed for Cuba would be boarded and searched.

As the quarantine went into effect and the hours ticked by, the chances for mistake and miscalculation grew by the minute. Khrushchev and Kennedy maintained almost daily communication. A possible break finally came in a long, emotional but balanced telegram from Khrushchev, in which he urged that he and Kennedy ought not to pull "the knot of war" so tight that they would not be able to untie it. For "then it will be necessary to cut that knot, and what that would mean is not for me to explain to you because you yourself understand perfectly of what terrible forces our countries dispose." Khrushchev said that he had lived through two wars and knew "that war ends when it has rolled through cities and villages, everywhere sowing death and destruction."

Kennedy and his colleagues on the Executive Committee felt a glimmer of optimism. But then came a second letter from the Russians, much more belligerent in tone, saying that the missiles from Cuba would be withdrawn only if the missiles in Turkey were withdrawn. Kennedy was angered by this reply, for he regarded it as a further threat. "We are now in an entirely new ball game," he said. United States leaders began to make plans for an air attack over Cuba, to begin the next morning and to be followed by an invasion. But there were some indications that the second letter was not from Khrushchev at all, but from the Soviet foreign office. Robert Kennedy suggested answering the first letter, ignoring the second. The President followed that advice, writing Khrushchev that he would promise not to invade Cuba if the missiles were withdrawn. Khrushchev accepted. Robert Kennedy, meanwhile, privately guaranteed that the missiles (obsolete in any event) would be withdrawn from Italy and Turkey. The crisis was over. The world relaxed.

The missile crisis was a public trauma, in some ways the most terrifying confrontation of the Cold War. It had many consequences. Both Kennedy and Khrushchev were shaken by their view from the brink into the abyss of a nuclear war. A nuclear test ban was negotiated in the summer of 1963. It was limited, however, to atmospheric tests and did not halt the spiraling arms race. The Chinese Communists attacked Khrushchev for cowardice, and the episode pushed the Chinese and the Russians further apart. Finally, Khrushchev's colleagues viewed the crisis as a further example of Khrushchev's "harebrained schemes." It started his downfall from power, which ended in the autumn of 1964 when Leonid Brezhnev and Alexsei Kosygin deposed the unpredictable Mr. K.

The domestic tension generated by United States attitudes toward Latin American was revealed when civil war broke out on April 25, 1965, in the desperately poor Dominican Republic. On one side in this civil war were the supporters of a military-civilian junta. Opposing them were the left-wing followers of Juan Bosch, the first democratically elected president of the Dominican Republic since 1924, who had been overthrown by the junta in September 1963. President Lyndon Johnson ordered 23,000 American troops to the island, the first such intervention since 1926. "The last thing I wanted — and the last thing the American people wanted — was another

Cuba on our doorstep," President Johnson recalled in his memoirs. He continued:

> The decisions I made on April 29 were as follows: First, that the danger of a Communist takeover in the Dominican Republic was a real and present one; second, that a Communist regime in the Dominican Republic would be dangerous to the peace and safety of the hemisphere and the United States; third, that danger still existed, in the disintegrating situation, for both Americans and foreign civilians in Santo Domingo. . . .

After a careful investigation by the Senate Foreign Relations Committee in 1965, Chairman J. William Fulbright concluded that the intervention was unjustified:

> Guided by a reflex bred into them by Fidel Castro, American policymakers have developed a tendency to identify revolution with communism, assuming because they have something to do with each other, as indeed they do, that they are one and the same thing, as indeed they are not. The pervading suspicion of social revolutionary movements on the part of United States policymakers is unfortunate indeed because there is the strong possibility of more explosions in Latin America. . . . The central fact about the intervention of the United States in the Dominican Republic was that we had closed our minds to the causes and to the essential legitimacy of revolution in a country in which democratic procedures had failed. The involvement of an undetermined number of communists in the Dominican revolution was judged to discredit the entire reformist movement, like poison in a well, and rather than use our considerable resources to compete with the communists for influence with the democratic forces who actively solicited our support, we intervened militarily on the side of a corrupt and reactionary military oligarchy. We thus lent credence to the idea that the United States is the enemy of social revolution, and therefore the enemy of social justice, in Latin America.

In 1970 a Marxist, Salvador Allende, was elected president of Chile by a minority vote in a closely contested three-man election. Allende nationalized the copper and utility companies owned by the United States and strengthened relations with the Kremlin. But he adhered to the democratic system, did not engage in international revolutionary activities, and tried to maintain steady relations with his more conservative neighbors. Economic conditions in Chile deteriorated under his rule, partly because the Nixon administration set hard terms for Chile on international economic and monetary matters. In September 1973, right-wing military officers carried out a coup in which Allende was killed, thus bringing to an end the long tradition of democracy that had set Chile off from most of its Latin American neighbors. In its place, the officers set up a repressive dictatorship, brutal even by Latin American standards.

Initially, the coup was thought to be a purely local affair. However, subsequent Congressional investigations revealed considerable anti-Allende activity, not only by private American corporations but also by the Nixon administration, which feared that Allende might become another Castro.

A special United States Senate Committee to Study Governmental Operations with Respect to Intelligence Activities came to some mixed but still disturbing conclusions in 1975:

> In 1970, the CIA engaged in another special effort, this at the express request of President Nixon. . . . The CIA attempted, directly, to foment a military coup in Chile. . . . When the coup attempt failed and Allende was inaugurated president, the CIA was authorized . . . to fund groups in opposition to Allende in Chile. The effort was massive. Eight million dollars was spent in the three years between the 1970 elections and the military coup in September 1973. Money was furnished to media organizations, to opposition political parties, and, in limited amounts, to private-sector organizations.

The Committee went on to add, however, that it had found "no evidence" that the United States was directly involved in the coup. It added:

> This report does not attempt to offer a final judgment on the political propriety, the morality, or even the effectiveness of American covert activity in Chile. . . . Was 1970 a mistake, an aberration? Or was the threat posed to the national security interests of the United States so grave that the government was remiss in not seeking his downfall directly during 1970–73? . . .

On these questions, Committee members may differ. So may American citizens. . . . Covert action has been perceived as a middle ground between diplomatic representation and the overt use of military force. In the case of Chile, that middle ground may have been far too broad.

The questions raised by the Committee were difficult and painful ones, questions for which the policies of the Cold War era can no longer provide sufficient answers. It will take several years of debate to develop new answers for the problems raised by our Latin American foreign policy. But the questions cannot be avoided.

VIETNAM AND
THE DOMINO THEORY

Vietnam was like a quagmire in a jungle. Each step taken by the United States was meant to put us on firmer ground and to help us get out. But each step only carried the United States more deeply into the muck. By November 1963, when an assassin's bullet felled President Kennedy in Texas, the United States was already entangled in the affairs of a country about which Americans knew little.

The first American to see Vietnam was an ocean-going peddler named Captain John Smith, who put into Saigon harbor more than a century ago. Disappointed that the only things he could sell were weapons, uniforms, and books, he put out to sea again and never went back. The entire region of Indochina was mostly ignored by Americans. It was colonized by the French. But during World War II, when the Japanese took control of the region, Americans began to take an interest in Indochina.

Shortly after the end of World War II, war broke out in Vietnam between the Viet Minh, the nationalist forces led by Communist Ho Chi Minh, and the French, who had returned to their colonies in Indochina. Initially, the United States reacted to this event with confusion. On the one hand, it was traditionally opposed to imperialism. (Ho had sent at least eight letters to Washington immediately after World War II asking United States assistance for the Vietnamese independence movement.) On the other hand, the United States wanted a strong, anti-Communist France in Europe, and the French insisted that they could not be strong without their colonies. The growing confrontation with the Soviet Union in Europe determined America's course. The United States decided to support France. As Secretary of State Dean Acheson once explained, "The French blackmailed us." By 1949 the United States was providing extensive military aid to the French through NATO, which they, in turn, used in Vietnam.

Mao's victory in China in 1949 and the start of the Korean War in 1950 convinced United States leaders that Vietnam had to be "saved" from communism at all costs. Shortly after the Korean War began, President Truman ordered an increase in American aid to the French for Vietnam, and by 1954 the United States was paying 70 percent of the French military budget. Traditional arguments against colonialism seemed much less important than what was considered a world-wide struggle against communism.

But the French were losing their grip. The longer they fought in Vietnam, the more united the people became against them. Their control rapidly slipping away, the French decided, in 1954, to make a last stand in an isolated valley at Dien Bien Phu. For two months the eyes of governments all over the world were glued on the beleaguered French garrison, under siege by the Viet Minh. The French requested American military intervention, and some top United States officials argued strongly that we should use atomic weapons to relieve the French and commit our own soldiers. After some hesitation, President Eisenhower decided against that course. Meanwhile, diplomats from the Western and Communist countries were meeting in Geneva, Switzerland, to see if some political solution might be found. The United States was a reluctant participant. Secretary of State Dulles even refused to shake hands with China's foreign minister Chou En-lai. (This was a slight not to be repaired until President Nixon met with Chou in Peking two decades later.) In the middle of the Geneva Conference, the French foreign minister was handed a note. He turned pale. Dien Bien Phu had fallen; the French role in Indochina was finished.

In a hurried effort to find some kind of compromise, the Conference finally produced the Geneva Agreements of July 1954. The United States refused to adhere publicly to the agreements; it merely "took note" of them.

First, a truce would occur between Ho's forces and the French. Second, the country was temporarily divided at the 17th parallel, with the French withdrawing from all territory north of that line. Third, neither North Vietnam nor South Vietnam would join any military alliances, nor would they allow any foreign bases on their soil. Fourth, national elections, supervised by a joint commission of representatives from India, Canada, and Poland, would be held within two years to unify the country. Fifth, the pro-Communist Pathet Lao forces would be allowed to regroup in neighboring Laos; and both Laos and Cambodia would become independent.

At that time, the Viet Minh controlled two-thirds of Vietnam, but in accepting the Geneva Agreements, Ho pulled his troops back into the northern half of the nation. President Eisenhower wrote in his memoirs: "I have never talked or corresponded with a person knowledgeable in Indochinese affairs who did not agree that, had elections been held as of the time of the fighting, possibly 80 percent of the population would have voted for the Communist Ho Chi Minh." Thus the first Vietnam War ended.

Even as the first war was ending, the grounds were being laid for the second Vietnam War. The National Security Council called the Geneva Agreements a "disaster." Accordingly, the United States began to take steps to retrieve the situation. In the field, it began a campaign of harassment and psychological warfare against the Communists. In Hanoi, the capital of Communist North Vietnam, secret agents of the Central Intelligence Agency (CIA) poured sugar into the engines of the city's buses in order to stall them. More important, the United States sent a small number of military advisers to help the anti-Communist government of South Vietnam, headed by Ngo Dinh Diem. John Foster Dulles took the lead in creating the Southeast Asia Treaty Organization (SEATO), right after the Geneva Conference in 1954. This organization was modeled on NATO and was supposed to contain communism in Asia, but there were important differences. At first, the only two real

Asian countries to sign up were the Philippines and Thailand, for it was unclear what SEATO provided beyond library and cultural exchanges and morale boosting.

According to the Geneva Agreements, elections to re-unify the two halves of Vietnam were to be held in 1956, but Diem, with American support, refused to participate. Initially, Diem had some popularity as an anti-Communist nationalist. As time went on, however, he lost the people's support. He opposed making any significant land reforms, and he attempted to destroy the traditional bases of authority, centered in the villages, to build his own power bases. Despite $1.8 billion in United States aid between 1954 and 1959, the country was neither economically nor politically secure. The Catholics, only 10 percent of the population, seemed to have a privileged position in a country that was more than 70 percent Buddhist. Diem and his immediate family, including the beautiful but acid-tongued Madame Nhu who was known as the "Dragon Lady," ruled increasingly by dictatorial methods. Responding to peasant unrest in the late 1950's, old elements of the Viet Minh, led by Communists, began to regroup under the new name, Viet Cong. By 1961, the Viet Cong controlled large parts of rural South Vietnam.

In an effort to cope with this situation, the United States, under President Kennedy, increased its already substantial aid to Vietnam. The number of United States military advisers there was increased from 400 to 15,000, making the United States commitment much stronger. This aid did little good; Diem refused to carry out the reforms suggested by the American advisers. Diem was anything but the "Winston Churchill of Southeast Asia," as Vice-President Lyndon Johnson had described him in 1961. In truth he was becoming an increasingly isolated and tyrannical dictator, who was losing his grip on the country.

The Viet Cong were not the only problem. Buddhist monks led widespread protests in the urban areas, a few even burning themselves to death in public. Diem promised the United States that he would make peace with the Buddhists. Instead, in August 1963, the Diem government cut the phone lines to the American offices and then launched attacks on Buddhist temples, shooting and killing many monks. When

Diem continued his terror, even jailing hundreds of high school students, the Kennedy administration decided it could no longer support his government. On November 1, 1963, Vietnamese army officers, with a green light from American officials, staged a successful coup. Diem and his brother were captured and shot in the back of a truck. With Diem out of the way, the United States became the most important political force in South Vietnam. South Vietnam was now, in effect, a dependent client state of the United States.

"Why are we in Vietnam?" was a question Americans would continually ask themselves throughout an anguished decade of military involvement. The immediate reasons for the transformation of the "limited-risk gamble" of the Eisenhower years into a major commitment were the application of the Containment Doctrine to Asia and a belief in the domino theory. President Eisenhower succinctly explained that theory in 1954: "You have a row of dominoes set up, you knock over the first one, and what happens to the last one is the certainty that it will go over very quickly. So you could have a beginning of a disintegration that would have the most profound influences." In other words, if Vietnam went Communist, many other countries would follow suit. "The loss of South Vietnam would make pointless any further discussion about the importance of Southeast Asia to the free world," declared Secretary of State Dean Rusk and Secretary of Defense Robert McNamara in a 1961 joint report. "We would have to face the near certainty that the remainder of Southeast Asia and Indonesia would move to a complete accommodation with communism, if not formal incorporation with the Communist bloc."

The specter of a Viet Cong victory brought back memories of the domestic tumult in the United States after the "loss" of China. Also, the strategic domino theory went hand-in-hand with "lessons" that policymakers had learned from the 1930's. Special emphasis was put on pointing out its analogy to Munich, when the British and the French failed to stand up to Hitler's demands for new territory in 1938. United States policymakers believed that aggression had to be met and stopped; otherwise, the task of resisting the aggressor would prove so much more costly in the future.

Behind these concerns lay confusion on two matters. The first was that a "shadow of power" was seen as a substantial force; or, more specifically, the importance of the Third World was overemphasized. As the old colonial empires completely collapsed in the 1950's and early 1960's, a host of new nations — many of them tiny and all of them underdeveloped — came into existence. Both the Americans and the Russians believed that they must try to win the allegiance of these new nations and link them to their respective blocs. The Third World became the new battleground of the Cold War. A "win" for one side was supposed to be an automatic "loss" for the other. The Americans spoke of "nation-building"; the Russians, of "national liberation." What neither side realized was that most of these new nations were hardly even countries; they were struggling with problems of disorganization, bitter tribal antagonisms, and grinding poverty. Many of them would prove to be more of a liability than an asset to whichever bloc "claimed" them. By the end of the 1960's, many would end up military dictatorships, in which the preservation of power was more important to the military officers than ideology. None of this was clear at the beginning of the 1960's; the Third World then appeared to be a substantial force.

On the other hand, Americans, well into the 1960's, thought that the substantial rift between the Soviet Union and Communist China was a mere shadow. Not realizing that a cataclysmic split had occurred in the unity of the Communist world, they assumed that the Viet Cong were merely agents of Moscow and its junior partner, Peking. If the split had been recognized, then United States policymakers might have seen the Viet Cong and their allies in North Vietnam as representatives of a nationalistic and a local communistic movement — comparable to Marshall Tito's in Yugoslavia — rather than as agents of international communism. Viewed in that context, the Viet Cong's dominance in South Vietnam would not have been so serious a threat.

The Sino-Soviet split had indeed changed certain aspects of the Cold War. The bitter enmity between China and Russia — of the kind that can only come between two ex-brethren arguing about who possesses the one and only true faith — had helped bring about an improvement in United States relations with both countries and a general easing of Cold War tensions. The rift partly reflected clashing national aspirations and serious disputes over as much as a million square miles of border territory. More important for the rest of the world was the competition between the Chinese and Russians for the leadership of the Communist world. Its roots go back to the late 1940's and Stalin's lukewarm support for what he called the "margarine Communists," that is, Mao and his followers.

The rift became much more visible a decade later. The Chinese considered Khrushchev, with his slogan of "peaceful co-existence," to be a revolutionary sell-out. Mao believed himself, after Stalin's death, to be the ideological leader of communism. The Chinese took further offense when the Russians, fearing that the Communist giant next door was a potential rival, dragged their feet on fulfilling their promise to help the Chinese gain nuclear capability. The split came into the open at the Communist meeting in June 1960, at Bucharest, when Khrushchev denounced Mao. According to Professor Adam Ulam, it happened as follows:

> The first open break between the Soviet Union and Communist China—i.e., before other Communist parties and leaders—took place in Bucharest in June 1960. It is too bad that Eisenhower could not have been present at this Communist enclave. He could have witnessed Khrushchev outdoing himself in his ravings and rantings behavior—this time against a man he had described as his good friend, Mao. The Chinese Communists, he screamed, were madmen and "left adventurists" who wanted to unleash a war. The Chinese answered him in kind. . . . In the meantime, the Soviets pulled out their experts from China. A dispute of such proportions and of such reverberations, before so large an audience, could not be kept secret anymore than Khrushchev's "secret speech" of 1956. But in the United States attention was riveted on other things. . . .

In November 1960, a summit meeting of eighty-one Communist parties convened in Moscow. The conference produced a declaration in favor of "wars of national liberation." This declaration was seen as a tactic to give at least an external appearance of unity in the Communist world. The meeting was marked by bitter exchanges between the Russian and Chinese comrades. China and Russia were already as much concerned about each other as a potential enemy as they were about the United States. Two months later, Khrushchev gave a famous speech endorsing "wars of national liberation." Kennedy was so disturbed by the speech that he read it aloud at a meeting of the National Security Council, shortly after becoming President. The Americans regarded this speech as a Russian declaration of war for control of the Third World, and set up counter-insurgency programs to meet the expected guerrilla-warfare challenge. It was in this context that United States policymakers evaluated the situation in Vietnam. For several years more, they continued to assume that Khrushchev had issued a challenge to the West, rather than having indulged in some fiery oratory as part of his battles with Mao for the leadership of the Communist world.

The Americans thus went into Vietnam not only armed with the most advanced technology; they were also equipped with high ideals, some lessons learned from the past, a strategic vision predicated on the domino theory, and the image of militant international communism as a challenge to the United States. None of these things, however, ever quite meshed with the situation in Indochina.

But it was another President, not John Kennedy, who would make that painful discovery. Kennedy, assassinated in Dallas on November 22, 1963, was succeeded to the Presidency by Lyndon Johnson, a tall Texan who gloried in "pressing the flesh," be it on the campaign trail or in the Senate cloakrooms. He held out a splendid vision of domestic reform that he called "The Great Society." He might have achieved it, for he had, as Senate Majority Leader in the 1950's, proved himself an instinctive master of national politics. His instincts in international politics were nowhere as good, unfortunately, for he was far less experienced in this arena and thus more susceptible to bad advice. Chester Cooper, a key Vietnam policymaker, has analyzed the situation thus:

President Johnson inherited more than "the dirty little war" in Vietnam. He inherited Kennedy's principal advisers on foreign affairs . . . he found himself with a "commitment" of uncertain specificity and duration, and he fell heir to what the press was already describing as a "credibility gap." But in those days, and indeed for the years to follow, many American military and civilian officials were supremely confident that "victory" was in sight. It seemed unconceivable that the lightly armed and poorly equipped Communist forces could maintain their momentum against, first, increasing amounts of American assistance to the Vietnamese Army and, subsequently, American bombing and combat forces. To those officials (including myself in late 1964 and early 1965), the Saigon-based correspondents were Cassandras and false prophets.

The coup against Diem, in November 1963, did not bring the hoped-for stability and reform. Over the next eighteen months there were ten different governments, with generals plotting coups and countercoups against each other in a struggle for power. Meanwhile, the strength of the Communists was steadily increasing; and the South Vietnamese army, despite American aid, was proving itself incompetent in battle with its Communist rivals. By autumn of 1964, South Vietnamese military officials admitted that there was a real danger the Viet Cong would succeed in cutting the country in two.

The Americn role changed yet again with the Tonkin Gulf incident. Early in 1964 the United States had begun secretly supporting harrassment raids against North Vietnam, by both South Vietnamese forces and some forces from Thailand. Half a year later, on August 2, 1964, the American destroyer *Maddox* was fired on as it steamed through the Gulf of Tonkin thirty miles off the coast of North Vietnam. Although the ship was in international waters, its sensitive radar antennae were trained on North Vietnam, as part of an intelligence-gathering exercise. Suddenly, in broad daylight, three North Vietnamese torpedo boats appeared and, without provocation, fired on the *Maddox*. The North Vietnamese were retaliating for secret United States-supported raids against their coast that had been made earlier. Apparently, the North Vietnamese thought that the *Maddox* was involved—though in fact it was on an unrelated mission and its captain did not even know of the previous raids up the coast. Two days later, the *Maddox* and another United States ship the *Turner Joy* reported further attacks. Although the second incident was seen at the time as an even more serious provocation, many senior policymakers later concluded that it was more likely the result of confusion and nervous tension than a serious attack by the North Vietnamese.

Nevertheless, the Johnson administration responded to the two "incidents" with a double offensive. First, American war planes were dispatched to make sixty-four bombing sorties over North Vietnam. Second, the administration won the Senate's endorsement of the Tonkin Gulf Resolution, by a vote of 88 to 2. This resolution, passed on August 7, 1964, authorized the President "to take all necessary measures to repel any armed attack against the forces of the United States and to prevent further aggression." It added that the United States was prepared, "as the President determines, to take all necessary steps, including the use of armed force, to assist any member or protocol state of the Southeast Asia Collective Defense Treaty requesting assistance in defense of its freedom."

The resolution became the cause of bitter argument in later years. People who had become opponents of the war (like Senator Fulbright who in fact floor-managed the passage of the resolution) argued that it was a limited document, that its passage had been speeded on the basis of unreliable information, and that Congress rather than the President retained the war-making powers. Successive administrations, however, insisted that the resolution was a blank check to do whatever was "necessary" in Vietnam.

In autumn 1964, there was a presidential election. Johnson, running as the peace candidate, charged that his opponent Senator Barry Goldwater—whose slogan was "Why Not Victory?"—would lead the country recklessly into war. Once elected in his own right, and by an overwhelming vote, Johnson felt more free to act in Vietnam. When the Viet Cong attacked an American barracks at Pleiku in the Central Highlands of South Vietnam, killing eight soldiers and wounding one hundred, the President responded by initiating a sustained air war against North Vietnam under the code name of Operation Rolling Thunder. It was time, said CIA Director John McCone, to "roll up our sleeves and get down to business."

In April 1965, the United States began sending combat

marines to Vietnam, marking the formal American entry into another Asian land war. The situation continued to grow worse; almost every week, the South Vietnamese army lost an infantry battalion, and the Viet Cong captured a district capital. By the end of the year, the United States had not only started B-52 bombing raids over the South, but it had also committed more than 180,000 troops to lead some 500,000 South Vietnamese soldiers in combat against about 100,000 Viet Cong guerillas and 40,000 regular North Vietnamese troops. After a brief pause in the bombing for a "peace offensive," the United States resumed the bombing in February 1966 at even greater intensity. The targets now included the port cities of Haiphong and Hanoi, in an unsuccessful effort to force North Vietnam to stop sending troops and aid to the Viet Cong in the South.

The war intensified. The number of individual American flights over North Vietnam was increased from 55,000 in 1965 to 148,000 in 1966; total bomb tonnage was quadrupled to 128,000 tons. Yet the bombing seemed to accomplish little. The CIA estimated that 80 percent of the casualities were civilians. The North Vietnamese began to burrow underground, and the population and industries of the cities were dispersed over the countryside. North Vietnam also continued to increase its support for the Viet Cong guerrillas in South Vietnam and to send increasing numbers of its own troops there.

The political situation in South Vietnam did not improve either. The Viet Cong still controlled much of the countryside; they would fade away during the day when American search-and-destroy missions approached, and then slip back into the villages during the night and reassert their control. Another Buddhist crisis erupted, threatening another civil war within the civil war.

In 1967, under pressure from the United States, the generals carried out an election. The winner was Nguyen Van Thieu, a shy, conservative general who had already maneuvered himself into power. Air Marshall Nguyen Cao Ky was elected vice-president. Ky had been the former president, but his flamboyant costumes and "Captain Midnight" style, plus a remark that Adolph Hitler was his hero, had made him unacceptable to the United States. Despite the generals' efforts to fix the results, a civilian, Truong Dihn Dzu, ran a strong second on a platform of negotiating with the Viet Cong. The next year he was sentenced by a military court to five years in prison for "actions harmful to the anti-Communist spirit of the people and the army."

The Americans now carried the brunt of the war. The increasing American role meant rising costs for the United States. Americans not only had to pay for the war; they had to live with the war-induced inflation. More directly, young men were being drafted into the army to fight in Vietnam, and the casualties started to mount sharply in 1966. Antiwar protests began on college campuses, with peaceful teach-ins and demonstrations. Opponents were also distressed by the nature of the war. The United States military responded to Viet Cong assassinations with technological fury, using such weapons as B-52 jets and napalm, a gasoline jelly which horribly burned its victims. There were increasing instances of American troops, frustrated by jungle warfare, indiscriminately turning their guns on civilians. In one famous case, an American platoon shot dead the entire population – men, women, and children – of a village called My Lai.

Participation in national protests increased. In October 1967, 500,000 people converged on the Pentagon in Washington, D.C., for a massive antiwar demonstration. The political atmosphere was heating up and some of the demonstrations began to turn violent and ugly. The bipartisan foreign policy consensus was beginning to fall apart.

Nothing better demonstrated the end of the Cold War consensus, which had shaped United States policy since the late 1940's, than the conflicting testimony on Vietnam before the Senate Foreign Relations Committee in 1966. Secretary of State Dean Rusk explained the reasons for pursuing the war in Vietnam:

> In March 1947, in connection with our then assistance to Greece, which was under guerrilla attack, President Truman stated: "I believe that it must be the policy of the United States to support free peoples who are resisting attempted subjugation by armed minorities or by outside pressures." That is the policy we are applying in Vietnam in connection with specific commitments which we have taken in connection with that country.

The heart of the problem in South Vietnam is the effort of North Vietnam to impose its will by force. For that purpose Hanoi has infiltrated into South Vietnam large quantities of arms and tens of thousands of trained and armed men, including units of the North Vietnamese regular army. It is that external aggression, which the North has repeatedly escalated, that is responsible for the presence of United States combat forces.

The United States has a clear and direct commitment to the security of South Vietnam against external attack. The integrity of our commitments is absolutely essential to the preservation of peace right around the globe. At stake also is the still broader question: whether aggression is to be permitted, once again, to succeed. We know from painful experience that aggression feeds on aggression.

A central issue in the dispute between the two leading Communist powers today is to what extent it is effective — and prudent — to use force to promote the spread of communism. If the bellicose doctrines of the Asian Communists should reap a substantial reward, the outlook for peace in this world would be grim indeed. The steady purpose of the United States is to build a world in which all nations — large and small, rich and poor — can progress in peace, secure against external interference. In Vietnam we shall continue to seek a peaceful solution — but we shall do what is necessary to assist the South Vietnamese to repel the aggression against them. As President Johnson put it just last week: "The door of peace must be kept wide open for all who wish to avoid the scourge of war, but the door of aggression must be closed and bolted if man himself is to survive."

The challenge in Vietnam demands the selective application of our United States military power in support of the forces of the government of Vietnam. There is no alternative — except defeat and surrender — in the absence of a willingness on the part of the other side to sit down and make a peace. . . .

Challenging this interpretation was George Kennan, "author" of the Containment Doctrine in 1946 and 1947 and later ambassador to Yugoslavia under President Kennedy:

. . . [I]f we were not already involved as we are today in Vietnam, I would know of no reason why we should wish to become so involved, and I could think of several reasons why we should wish not to. Vietnam is not a region of major military, industrial importance. It is difficult to believe that any decisive developments of the world situation would be determined in normal circumstances by what happens on that territory. If it were not for the considerations of prestige that arise precisely out of our present involvement, even a situation in which South Vietnam was controlled exclusively by the Viet Cong, while regrettable, and no doubt morally unwarranted, would not, in my opinion, present dangers great enough to justify our direct military intervention.

Given the situation that exists today in the relations among the leading Communist powers, and by that I have, of course, in mind primarily the Soviet-Chinese conflict, there is every likelihood that a Communist regime in South Vietnam would follow a fairly independent course. There is no reason to suspect that such a regime would find it either necessary or desirable in present circumstances to function simply as a passive puppet and instrument of Chinese power. And as for the danger that its establishment there would unleash similar tendencies in neighboring countries, this, I think, would depend largely on the manner in which it came into power. . . .

But at the same time, I have great misgivings about any deliberate expansion of hostilities on our part directed to the achievement of something called "victory," if by the use of that term we envisage the complete disappearance of the recalcitrance with which we are now faced, the formal submission by the adversary to our will, and the complete realization of our present stated political aims. I doubt that these things can be achieved even by the most formidable military successes.

There seems to be an impression that if we bring sufficient military pressure to bear, there will occur at some point something in the nature of a political capitulation on the other side. I think this is a most dangerous assumption. . . .

Any total rooting-out of the Viet Cong from the territory of South Vietnam could be achieved, if it could be achieved at all, only at the cost of a degree of damage to civilian life and of civilian suffering, generally, for which I would not like to see this country responsible. . . .

It is clear that however justified our action may be in our own eyes, it has failed to win either enthusiasm or confidence even among people normally friendly to us. Our motives are widely misinterpreted, and the spectacle — the spectacle emphasized and reproduced in thousands of press photographs and stories that appear in the press of the world, the spectacle of Americans inflicting grievous injury on the lives of a poor and helpless people, and particularly a people of different race and color, no matter how warranted by military necessity or by the excesses of the adversary our operations may seem to us to be or may genuinely be — this spectacle produces reactions among millions of people throughout the world profoundly detrimental to the image we would like them to hold of this country. I am not saying that this is just or right. I am saying that this is so, and that it is bound in the circumstances to be so, and a victory purchased at the price of further such damage would be a hollow one in terms of our world interests, no matter what advantages it might hold from the standpoint of developments on the local scene.

Kennan had no sympathy for the Viet Cong, but he questioned the ability of the United States to intervene successfully.

> . . . I am trying to look at this whole problem not from the moral standpoint but from the practical one. I see in the Viet Cong a band of ruthless fanatics, partly misled, perhaps by the propaganda that has been drummed into them, but cruel in their purposes, dictatorial and oppressive in their aims. I am not conscious of having any sympathy for them. I think their claim to represent the people of South Vietnam is unfounded and arrogant and outrageous. A country which fell under this exclusive power would have my deepest sympathy, and I would hope that this eventuality at any rate would be avoided by a restrained and moderate policy on our part in South Vietnam. But, our country should not be asked, and should not ask of itself, to shoulder the main burden of determining the political realities in any other country, and particularly not in one remote from our shores, from our culture, and from the experience of our people.
>
> This is not only not our business but I don't think we can do it successfully. . . . It is not so that when men call themselves Communists, some sort of magic transportation takes place within them which makes them wholly different from other human beings or from what they were before. Feelings of nationalism, ordinary feelings, still affect them to a large extent. I think these — this reality plays a part in all of Vietnam. I don't think they want domination by the Chinese.

Despite the domestic debate, by the autumn of 1967 American military leaders were optimistically predicting that they saw "the light at the end of the tunnel." General Westmoreland, the

American commander in Vietnam, declared in November that he was "never more encouraged in my four years in Vietnam."

The American role in the war by this time was awesome. Forty percent of America's combat-ready divisions, half of our tactical airpower, a third of our naval strength—altogether some 480,000 men—were fighting the war in Southeast Asia. The annual cost was $25 billion. The number of Americans killed in action between 1961 and 1966 was 6,500. In 1967 the number went to 9,000, with an additional 60,000 wounded. All this money and effort, it was assumed, would bring about an end to the war.

This bubble of United States optimism was punctured on January 31, 1968, when the Viet Cong and North Vietnamese launched their Tet (New Year) Offensive, an onslaught against dozens of cities and towns throughout South Vietnam. The Communist forces even succeeded in entering the American embassy in Saigon. Heavy fighting continued for a month. While the attacks were costly to the Communists—they suffered perhaps 40,000 dead, compared to 4,000 for the Americans and 5,000 for the South Vietnamese army—they succeeded in striking a blow that almost toppled the structure of power in South Vietnam. Moreover, American prestige and self-confidence was seriously damaged. The American people, seeing the Tet Offensive unfold nightly on their news shows, were shocked. For many Americans, the war seemed to have lost all reason. The ultimate insanity was the film of American planes bombing—not Hanoi—but Saigon, the capital of South Vietnam, in an effort to dislodge Communist guerrillas who had entered by city by bicycle and pushcart.

In the aftermath of the Tet Offensive, General Westmoreland requested an additional 200,000 troops. Not only was the request turned down but Washington began a review of its entire commitment. President Johnson was stunned by the major setback, if not outright failure, that the Tet Offensive represented for his policy in Vietnam.

Domestically, Johnson was also being pressured by the rising tide of public protest and, specifically, by Senators Robert Kennedy and Eugene McCarthy, who were challenging his renomination by advancing antiwar planks. In March, Johnson called in a group of elder statesmen, whom he called the "wise old men," to help him review policy. The most distinguished of these men was Dean Acheson, who had been Secretary of State under President Truman, a member of President Kennedy's Executive Committee during the Cuban Missile Crisis, and was intimately associated with the Containment Doctrine. The President was shaken when Acheson said that he had lost faith in the Defense Department's briefings. "With all due respect, Mr. President, the Joint Chiefs of Staff don't know what they're talking about," he said during one luncheon.

A few days later, the group of "wise old men" met with the President in the family dining room of the White House. It was another of those deadly serious high councils, which had been held during every crisis in the Cold War in the last quarter century. But, for the first time, one such council recommended that the President do less, not more. Dean Acheson, sitting at the President's right, summarized the general attitude when he said that the American objectives could not be achieved within the limits of time and resources allowed by the American people. "This fact," said Acheson, "together with our broader interests in Southeast Asia, and Europe in connection with the dollar crisis, requires a decision now to disengage within a limited time." He added, "One thing seems sure—the old slogan that success is just around the corner won't work."

Johnson was shocked by this advice from the men who had initiated America's Cold War policy. He reluctantly began the arduous process of disengagement. On March 31 he went on nationwide television to announce that the bombing over North Vietnam would be severely restricted and that the United States would soon begin negotiations with the enemy. Then, in a political bombshell, he took himself out of contention for the 1968 presidential election. Many people had thought, when Johnson won his overwhelming mandate in 1964, that he might prove himself one of America's greatest Presidents. It was his personal tragedy that, instead, he had become bogged down in the quicksands of Vietnam. The war in Indochina destroyed his political career and left him a haggard, frustrated, and defeated man during the rest of his term. The negotiations, which began in Paris in May 1968, dragged on fruitlessly through the last days of the Johnson administration.

Richard Nixon, rebounding from his 1960 defeat, won the

Presidency against Hubert Humphrey in 1968. During his campaign, he pledged himself to "bring us together" by ending the American role in Vietnam and by healing the bitter domestic divisions. Six months after his inauguration, he enunciated the "Nixon Doctrine," during a stopover at the small Pacific island of Guam on his way to Asia. In contrast with the straightforward Truman Doctrine, which had proclaimed the Containment Policy, the Nixon Doctrine seemed to have two meanings. The President clearly opposed United States participation in further land wars in Asia; but Nixon left no doubt that he intended to maintain a major American role in Southeast Asia. Later the President explained that his doctrine bespoke "a revised policy of involvement," which meant both an end to intervention under the Containment Policy and continued intervention.

The Nixon administration pursued this two-headed policy under the name of "Vietnamization." The slow withdrawal of American ground forces was begun, while the United States continued to supply vast amounts of aid to the Thieu regime, including enough aircraft to give South Vietnam the third largest air force in the world after the United States and the Soviet Union. The United States continued to "fight" on through its South Vietnam ally but without incurring the unpopular American casualties. The negotiations in Paris, with the added participation of the Viet Cong and South Vietnam, ground on with no results.

Domestic opposition was beginning to fade away, although it briefly flared to life again in April and May of 1970 when the Nixon administration attempted to extend the ground war by ordering American troops into neighboring Cambodia. Bowing to the surge of protest, the President withdrew the forces in June. Responding to another big North Vietnamese and Viet Cong offensive in 1972, the United States renewed the air war over North Vietnam and also mined the harbor of Haiphong, the major port of North Vietnam. In the midst of this response, the last American combat forces were withdrawn from Vietnam.

In the first four years of the Nixon Administration, United States relations with the Soviet Union and China dramatically improved. Washington came to realize that Hanoi was independent of the two Communist giants. Why, then, if American policymakers no longer saw the war as an effort to contain international communism, did the United States continue to put such emphasis on the survival of the regime of General Thieu, who had assumed dictatorial powers and did not seem to be a popular leader? The question had been answered in 1969 by Henry Kissinger, the former Harvard professor who had become Nixon's chief foreign-policy adviser. "However we got into Vietnam, whatever the judgment of our actions, ending the war honorably is essential for the peace of the world." As in the Kennedy and Johnson years, an "honorable end" meant the continuation of the Saigon regime. In other words—as argued by Nixon and Kissinger—the United States would lose its credibility as a great power in the eyes of the rest of the world if it suffered a public "defeat" in Indochina after the years of involvement, and at the hands of guerrillas and soldiers of a backward peasant country. And if the United States lost its credibility, then other countries would be tempted to test their will and power against ours, and the United States would be exposed to even greater dangers and instability. The Nixon Administration spent its entire first four years "ending" the war in Vietnam—a longer period than it took the United States to fight World War II.

It fell to Kissinger finally to make a makeshift peace. Flying secretly to Paris innumerable times, he conferred often with Le Duc Tho, a member of North Vietnam's ruling Politburo. By the autumn of 1972, the two men seemed to have reached an agreement. Kissinger's announcement a few days before the 1972 presidential election that "peace is at hand" is credited with helping Nixon to overwhelm his challenger, Senator George McGovern, and carry forty-nine states.

Peace, however, was not quite at hand. Both North and South Vietnam balked at some of the terms Kissinger and Nixon wanted. To bring the South Vietnamese around, the United States used some backstage arm-twisting. To pressure the North Vietnamese, the United States unleashed on them a massive, twelve-day Christmas bombing campaign. Finally, in January 1973, an agreement was signed in Paris. In presenting it to the American people, Henry Kissinger declared, "It should be clear by now that no one in the war has had a monopoly of anguish and that no one in these debates has had a monopoly of moral insight."

The terms of the agreement were ambiguous and obviously of a temporary nature. The full irony of the agreement became clear in October 1973 when Henry Kissinger and Le Duc Tho were jointly awarded the Nobel Peace Prize. By then, few could doubt that the agreement was little more than a disguise under which both sides would continue the struggle.

The tempo of war accelerated throughout 1974, with both sides acting more and more as if the agreement had never existed. The end was nearing. In the spring of 1975, the Viet Cong and North Vietnamese launched an offensive and began to capture the provincial capitals. The South Vietnamese army, despite years of training by the Americans and the billions of dollars' worth of American equipment, had lost its direction and will to fight. It simply collapsed, and its soldiers fled, panic-stricken, in front of the advancing Viet Cong and North Vietnamese armies. By mid-April, neighboring Cambodia had fallen to the Khmer Rouge (the Cambodian equivalent of the Viet Cong). On April 28, President Gerald Ford ordered an emergency evacuation of Saigon. Helicopters swept back and forth between the city and waiting aircraft carriers, bearing out the last Americans and several thousand Vietnamese. On April 30, 1975, Saigon surrendered. The Indochina War was over.

How are we to measure the results? In numbers, 56,000 Americans and probably two million Vietnamese and Cambodians died, and 15 million, out of a total population of 28 million, were made refugees. It will take years to know the full consequences of these Communist victories in Southeast Asia. From all accounts, the Khmer Rouge immediately instituted a savage dictatorship in Cambodia, driving most of the urban population—even the sick and the aged—from the cities. The old border between South and North Vietnam is meaningless. How the new rulers will govern Vietnam is less clear. They appear to be more sophisticated and less doctrinaire than their new Cambodian neighbors. Although the Vietnamese victors are Communists, they are also fierce nationalists, and they face their own problem of keeping in balance their relations with those two bitter rivals, Moscow and Peking.

The Vietnam War is something that Americans want to forget; but painful as the experience was, some lessons cannot be ignored. American power, like all power, is limited; some things it can do, others it cannot. Commitments cannot be made lightly. In addition, we have learned that there are different kinds of Communists: Some are more independent of Moscow than others; some are more tyrannical than others. And we know, too, that nationalism can be as powerful a weapon as Marxism.

When the Vietnam War began, it was widely supported by the American public; by the end, however, it had almost no support. The war was a traumatic experience for the American people, and it had shaken their confidence in our country's institutions and leadership. To make matters worse, the ending of the war coincided with one of the most serious political crises in our history, the Watergate Affair. The American people learned that during the administration of President Richard Nixon, there had been a widespread pattern — reaching right up to the White House — of illegal activities, Constitutional violations, and major financial irregularities, which were practiced to ensure the reelection of Nixon and to hurt as much as possible the "enemies" of the White House. All of these acts, in retrospect, were hardly necessary, for Richard Nixon almost surely would have been reelected by a large vote in 1972 without resorting to any of the gross and unethical behavior that Watergate revealed. As it was, the President's own behavior, including his participation in the Watergate "cover-up" (as revealed by the secret tape recordings Nixon had made of his own conversations), forced him to resign in disgrace — the first time in our history that a President had ever resigned. He was succeeded by Gerald Ford, who had shortly before become Vice-President. Ford had replaced Vice President Spiro Agnew, who had been forced to resign after his involvement in corrupt practices was uncovered.

The ending of the Vietnam War, combined with Watergate, raised major doubts in the public mind about the integrity of many governmental institutions and procedures. One established institution, the Central Intelligence Agency, a semisecret organization that was once an unquestioned instrument of Cold War politics, found itself being spotlighted by Congressional investigations and having to defend its reputation. Certainly, the disaster in Vietnam called for a new reevaluation of America's role in the world. And in truth, the reevaluation had already begun.

"DETENTE"

By the early 1970's, it was clear that a new world was at hand. Political leaders from both sides of the iron curtain no longer talked of the inevitable enmity between communistic and democratic states but rather of "detente" and "peaceful coexistence" and businesslike relations. At first, it was strange to hear such unfrosty words from the lips of Richard Nixon. Ever since he had come to Washington as a young Congressman in the 1940's, in the early days of the Cold War, Nixon's career had been closely identified with anti-communism. His opposition to communism had not dimmed over a generation, but the changes in the world were unmistakable. President Nixon's State of the World message in 1970 contained what was virtually an obituary for the Cold War era:

The postwar period in international relations has ended.

Then, we were the only great power whose society and economy had escaped World War II's massive destruction. Today the ravages of that war have been overcome. Western Europe and Japan have recovered their economic strength, their political vitality, and their national self-confidence. Once the recipients of American aid, they have now begun to share their growing resources with the developing world. Once almost totally dependent on American military power, our European allies now play a greater role in our common policies, commensurate with their growing strength.

Then, new nations were being born, often in turmoil and uncertainty. Today, these nations have a new spirit and a growing strength of independence. Once, many feared that they would become simply a battleground of cold-war rivalry and fertile ground for Communist penetration. But this fear misjudged their pride in their national identities and their determination to preserve their newly won sovereignty.

Then, we were confronted by a monolithic Communist world. Today, the nature of that world has changed—the power of individual Communist nations has grown, but international Communist unity has been shattered. Once a unified bloc, its solidarity has been broken by the powerful forces of nationalism. The Soviet Union and Communist China, once bound by an alliance of friendship, had become bitter adversaries by the mid-1960's. The only times the Soviet Union has used the Red Army since World War II have been against its own allies—in East Germany in 1953, in Hungary in 1956, and in Czechoslovakia in 1968. The Marxist dream of international Communist unity has disintegrated.

Then, the United States had a monopoly or overwhelming superiority of nuclear weapons. Today, a revolution in the technology of war has altered the nature of the military balance of power. New types of weapons present new dangers. Communist China has acquired thermonuclear weapons. Both the Soviet Union and the United States have acquired the ability to inflict unacceptable damage on the other, no matter which strikes first. There can be no gain and certainly no victory for the power that provokes a thermonuclear exchange. Thus, both sides have recognized a vital mutual interest in halting the dangerous momentum of the nuclear arms race.

Then, the slogans formed in the past century were the ideological accessories of the intellectual debate. Today, the "isms" have lost their vitality—indeed the restlessness of youth on both sides of the dividing line testifies to the need for a new idealism and deeper purposes.

This is the challenge and the opportunity before America as it enters the 1970's.

The world of the 1970's looked different. Instead of a bipolar world, there was now a "pentagonal world" of five main powers —Western Europe, Japan, and China had joined the United

States and the Soviet Union in the international cast of stars. Many changes had occurred in the late 1960's and early 1970's to blur the confrontation between the American and Soviet blocs, which had been the basic condition of the Cold War.

The Sino-Soviet dispute had made Russia eager to relieve the tensions on its western borders and to secure a general ratification of the status quo in Europe. (That the West recognized the Soviet sphere had been yet again made clear in August 1968, when the West stood by as Russian tanks rolled into Czechoslovakia to overturn an independent leadership that was moving to democratize its Communist government.) Russia also wanted to improve relations with the West because it needed foreign technology to improve its economy. And, for an added benefit, the Russians hoped that getting Western and Japanese aid in developing the natural resources of Siberia would frustrate Chinese efforts to claim some of that vast, underpopulated region for itself. That the people of the Soviet Union thirsted for Western consumer goods was proved by the great welcome they gave Pepsi-Cola when it came to Russia!

Chancellor Willy Brandt of West Germany also sought to end unnecessary tensions in Europe. Pursuing his *Ostpolitik* (East Policy), he negotiated treaties with the Soviet Union and Poland, which recognized the territorial changes made at Yalta and Potsdam. He received the Nobel Peace Prize for his efforts, which, ironically, had aroused considerable opposition among extreme nationalists in his own country. Brandt also opened a dialogue with East Germany, citing the formula of "two German states in one German nation." In 1973, just twenty-eight years after the Allied coalition defeated Hitler's Germany, the two Germany's of the Cold War were finally accepted into the United Nations Organization. In other words, after more than a quarter of a century, the division of Germany and Europe brought about by World War II was formally accepted by both sides. By that acceptance a major source of fear and insecurity was alleviated, and improved relations and widened contacts between East and West became possible.

European stability and acceptance of the status quo was underwritten further at the European Security Conference, which convened in Helsinki at the end of July 1975. With thirty-five heads of state in attendance, including President

Gerald Ford and Leonid Brezhnev, it was, in effect, the long-postponed peace conference that had never been held after World War II. The borders, as "written" by the Allied armies in the last months of World War II, were at last officially accepted by all parties. This acceptance had been a major Russian goal. In turn, the Russians were reluctantly forced to commit themselves, generally, to freer contacts between East and West and to a greater recognition of basic human rights. (It will take years to know how well the Russians have lived up to their promises, if at all.) Brezhnev also said, forcefully, that "no one should try to dictate to other peoples, on the basis of foreign-policy considerations of one kind or another, the manner in which they ought to manage their internal affairs." His remarks were painfully ironic in the light of the fact that the use of Soviet tanks to crush the liberalization movement in Czechoslovakia in 1968 had been justified in the name of the "Brezhnev Doctrine."

In addition to this new stability, there was another major change in Western Europe. Great Britain, at last realizing that its future lay in Europe and not with the fading remnants of its empire, joined the Common Market (European Economic Community, or EEC) on January 1, 1973. With the addition of Ireland and Denmark as well, the Common Market now included nine nations operating as one productive, highly industrialized economic giant. While the Common Market was primarily an economic rather than a political entity, it was nevertheless recognized as a brawny newcomer in the field of international politics. By the mid-1970's, the Common Market nations were trying to shape a common foreign policy.

The development of the Common Market points to another major change, a change in economic relations. The devaluations and continued weakness of the American dollar in the early 1970's were not only evidence of an unstable, complex international monetary system but were also testimony to the fact that the United States no longer dominated the world economy in the way it had from the mid-1940's through the end of the 1960's. America's Cold War allies, Japan and Western Europe, were now our leading economic rivals, as well as partners. Western Europe (and Russia, for that matter) had surpassed the United States in the production of steel, and Japan was not far behind. Markets, natural resources, and technology were becoming more urgent matters than ideology. The Western nations now had to make greater efforts to find ways to "manage" their political and economic interdependence.

Also emerging were other problems that lay outside the framework of the Soviet-American confrontation. For instance, the Arab attack on Israel, in October 1973, led to a major Middle East war. In order to pressure the Western states who were friendly to Israel—or at least neutral—the Arab oil producers placed an embargo on the shipment of oil to the Western nations. This, in turn, led to the price of oil skyrocketing; the high prices were maintained and raised even further by the Organization of Petroleum Exporting Countries (OPEC) after the embargo had ended. Although this price rise was hard on the Western economies, it was devastating to the more fragile economies of the developing nations. It shifted a great amount of wealth and political power to the oil producers, and it heightened the tensions between the Northern and Southern Hemispheres of the globe. In this major new problem, which put economic matters at the top of the international agenda, the Soviet Union and other Communist states played a relatively small part.

Another new problem was the proliferation of nuclear capability—that is, the ability of an increasing number of nations to develop or purchase their own nuclear weapons. This is one of the most frightening problems that the world must deal with in this last quarter of the twentieth century. For it is a situation that promotes instability on a grand scale. It now becomes possible that a border dispute between two developing nations, each possessing a small nuclear arsenal, could trigger off a world conflagration. The Soviet Union and the United States are realizing that they share a strong common interest in finding some method to restrain the spread of nuclear weapons.

Finally, there was the change in United States domestic attitudes toward foreign policy. No longer can United States leaders count on broad public support for the kinds of foreign-policy initiatives and interventions that occurred at the height of the Cold War. Many Americans came to believe, in the aftermath of the Vietnam trauma, that there are limits to what the United States can and should try to do, that our country has problems at home which need solutions before we try to solve problems in distant parts of the world. Politicians who ignore this new constraint risk domestic tumult and perhaps, as Lyndon Johnson discovered, an end to their political career. Congress, in particular, is less willing to hand out "blank checks" to the President, whether those checks be in the form of appropriations or in declarations like the Tonkin Gulf Resolution. Many Senators and Representatives who opposed the Vietnam War blamed themselves for surrendering their rights to the President and argue that the Executive has become too powerful in the conduct of foreign affairs. They have sought to reassert the Constitutional system of checks-and-balances. Although the President still continues to hold the bulk of power, these domestic pressures force him to pursue a more cautious foreign policy.

Within this context of change, the United States had to take, as President Nixon would say, a "lower profile" in the world. His administration guided the nation from Cold War confrontations toward negotiations. The President broadened United States contacts with the Soviet Union. At the same time, he opened a dialogue with China. It was now thought in Washington that China had been something of a "paper tiger" during the Cold War, issuing revolutionary proclamations to cover the economic backwardness and weakness of that teeming country. In the "pentagonal world," the Containment Policy was discarded in favor of a new policy — balance of power. No longer did the United States and Russia see international politics as a zero-sum game. There were no absolute friendships nor any absolute hostilities; only the five major powers pursuing their own interests with some prudence and self-restraint, and some respect for the interests of their rivals. Both the Soviet Union and the United States were retreating from their universal goals: Russia was not trying to communize the world, and America was not trying to make the world over in its own image. It seemed that diversity and peaceful coexistence might in fact be possible.

This new relationship between the United States and the Soviet Union was referred to as "detente." By the mid-1970's, there was considerable confusion in the United States about the meaning of detente. Some people were charging that its benefits had been oversold and that the expectations for a "generation of peace" had been much exaggerated.

What does detente mean? First, it involves making somewhat more explicit some of the "rules" of the Cold War that had only been implied: Neither side will push too hard into any areas of vital interest to the other; each will make some effort to contain crises; both sides will cooperate in avoiding nuclear war. Also, detente involves some degree of cooperation in certain areas, such as controlling the arms race, curbing nuclear proliferation, preventing pollution of the environment, and trade. Detente has also meant increased communication between the United States and the Soviet Union, at both a policy and a cultural level. Finally, detente is a matter of atmospheric change —an alteration in the psychological climate, a reduction in the state-of-alarm tensions, a softening of the harsh rhetoric of the Cold War.

But detente does not mean that the competition between the Soviet Union and the United States for world leadership is over. Nor can we assume that the Russian leaders will abandon their dictatorial system of power.

Although the seeds of detente were planted in the 1960's, detente was not formally recognized until the Moscow summit meeting in May 1972, at which President Nixon and Leonid Brezhnev, the Soviet Communist Party's General Secretary, signed a "Basic Principles of Relations" agreement for the two nations. The two countries—each of them possessing thousands upon thousands of nuclear warheads—made some slow, tortuous progress in the SALT meetings. SALT stands for Strategic Arms Limitation Talks, and they are meant to put a cap on the expensive and dangerous arms race, particularly in regard to nuclear weapons and missiles. But these negotiations are extraordinarily complex; and, while certain important steps have been taken, there are many ambiguities and no shortage of critics. Other contacts have been increased, especially the trade between the Superpowers, but it has been marked by many controversies. Perhaps the best hope for detente was symbolized in July 1975 when—as seen on television sets around the world—American and Soviet spacecrafts linked up for two days in outer space, and the astronauts from the two adversary nations shook hands. Back on earth, however, one could not say that the Cold War had actually been buried. Even if the peoples of the Soviet Union had become somewhat less isolated from the West, and the Soviet leaders somewhat more responsive to world public opinion, nevertheless, there still was wide disquiet. For instance, the United States was concerned about the reasons behind the rapid build-up of the Soviet navy, as well as the Russian eagerness to meddle in a civil war in Angola in Southern Africa, which lay far outside the Soviet sphere.

It is too soon to write the obituary for the Cold War. At best, we are in a transition period, a time of thaw in the Cold War between East and West. Jimmy Carter, who was elected President of the United States in 1976, faces the complex task of adjusting U.S. foreign policy to a wide range of difficult new problems: nuclear proliferation, control of the ocean's resources, and the role of multinational corporations in international politics. The new generation of Russian leaders will also have to deal with unfamiliar problems. But the "pentagonal world" is still more a prediction for the future than a fact; the dividing line between East and West is blurred but not gone. A new crisis could once again polarize the world. For instance, in the Middle East, the United States and Russia could be dragged by their respective small allies into a confrontation that neither Superpower wants. A change of leadership in any of the major countries could also reverse the march toward peaceful coexistence.

Nevertheless, the world has survived the worst moments of the Cold War and reached a point where the end of the Cold War could be in sight. That itself is something that many people feared would never happen. No nation has won nor lost the Cold War. Rather, what began as a confrontation in the rubble of postwar Europe became a world-wide nuclear stand-off. Gradually, both the United States and the Soviet Union have become more secure and cautiously more confident in their respective positions. In more of such relaxation lies the best hope for a more durable peace in the future.

Bibliography

The most detailed study of the Cold War, *The Cold War and Its Origins, 1917-1960* (2 vols., Garden City, N.Y.: Doubleday, 1961), is by Denna F. Fleming of Vanderbilt University. Professor Fleming begins his account with the Bolshevik Revolution, and he consciously sets out to present the Soviet view. His volumes are particularly valuable as reference tools, for no dates, events, or movements of significance have escaped his net. Briefer, and very good, is John Lukacs' *A History of the Cold War* (Garden City, N.Y.: Anchor paperback, 1962). This richly interpretive volume is written by a college professor who knows both American and Russian history, a rarity in this day of specialization. Also very good, and midway in length between Lukacs and Fleming, is W. W. Rostow's *The United States in the World Arena: An Essay in Recent History* (New York: Harper, 1960). In many ways the best of the three, this analysis is by a professional economist who is concerned with the question of whether there is a "national style." The fact that Rostow was one of President Kennedy's personal advisers gives his ideas added interest.

Three other general histories also are worth reading. John W. Spanier's *American Foreign Policy Since World War II* (New York: Praeger paperback, 1960) ignores Latin America but otherwise is thorough. Spanier, from the University of Florida, also has written *The Truman-MacArthur Controversy and the Korean War* (Cambridge, Mass.: Harvard University Press, 1959), and is an exponent of the "realist" school of diplomacy. Norman A. Graebner's *Cold War Diplomacy: American Foreign Policy, 1945-1960* (Princeton: Anvil paperback, 1962) contains seven related essays and twelve key documents. Graebner also takes the "realist" line. Two journalists, Deane and David Heller, have written a popular account, *The Cold War* (Derby, Conn.: Monarch paperback, 1962). These analyses should be read in conjunction with George F. Kennan's near-classic *American Diplomacy, 1900-1950* (New York: Mentor paperback, 1952). Opposed to the "realist" view are Thomas I. Cook and Malcolm Moos's *Power through Purpose* (Baltimore: Johns Hopkins Press, 1955) and Frank Tannenbaum's *The American Tradition in Foreign Policy* (Norman: University of Oklahoma Press, 1955) which argue for a program of idealism. Ernest Lefever's *Ethics and*

United States Foreign Policy (New York: Meridian paperback, 1958) also is excellent. *An Uncertain Trumpet*, edited by Norman A. Graebner (New York: McGraw-Hill, 1962), contains highly readable articles on Stettinius, Byrnes, Acheson, and Dulles, and brings out the way personalities affect foreign policy.

There are many analyses of more specific subjects. On Yalta, see John L. Snell, ed., *The Meaning of Yalta* (Baton Rouge: Louisiana State University Press, 1956), and Richard F. Fenno, Jr., ed., *The Yalta Conference* (Boston: D. C. Heath, 1955). Fenno's analysis is one of the books in the "Problems in American Civilization" series. On China and Asia consult David N. Rowe, *Modern China* (Princeton: Anvil paperback, 1959), John K. Fairbank, *The United States and China* (new revised and enlarged edition, Cambridge, Mass.: Compass paperback, 1962), Edwin O. Reischauer, *The United States and Japan* (revised edition, Cambridge, Mass.: Compass paperback, 1962), Robert C. Bone, *Contemporary Southeast Asia* (New York: Random House paperback, 1962), and Kenneth Scott Latourette, *The American Record in the Far East, 1945-1951* (New York: Macmillan, 1952). On Berlin there are two excellent paperbacks: John Mander, *Berlin: Hostage for the West* (Baltimore: Penguin, 1962), and Charles B. Robson, ed., *Berlin: Pivot of Destiny* (New York: Ballantine, 1960). For the best, most thorough analyses of the subjects which their titles cover, one cannot better Herbert Feis's excellent works: *The Road to Pearl Harbor: The Coming of the War between the United States and Japan* (Princeton: Princeton University Press, 1950), and *Churchill, Roosevelt, Stalin* (Princeton: Princeton University Press, 1957).

On questions relating to nuclear warfare, the best analyses are Henry A. Kissinger, *Nuclear Weapons and Foreign Policy* (Garden City, N.Y.: Anchor paperback, 1958), Bernard Brodie, *Strategy in the Missile Age* (Princeton: Princeton University Press, 1959), and Robert E. Osgood, *Limited War* (Chicago: University of Chicago Press, 1957). On Latin America, *The United States and Latin America* (New York: American Assembly paperback 1959), edited by Herbert L. Matthews, has some merit, and Robert J. Alexander, *Today's Latin America* (Garden City, N.Y.: Anchor paperback, 1962), is informative. For an understanding of the Kennedy administration one can begin with Theodore H. White, *The Making of the President 1960* (New York: Pocket Books, 1961).

Index

Acheson, Dean, 32, 37, 38, 46, 75, 90
Allende, Salvador, 71-72
Alliance for Progress, 66-67
Allies, 5, 6, 13, 14
Alperovitz, Gar, quoted 15-16
Ambrose, Stephen, quoted 42-43
American ideology, 19-20
Atlantic Charter, 8
atom bomb, 15, 17, 36
Austria, 54, 61
Axis powers, 5
balance of power (policy), 100
Baruch plan, 29
"Basic Principles of Relations" agreement, 101
Batista, Fulgencio, 64-65
Bay of Pigs, 67
Bevin, Ernest, 27, 34
bipolar world, 18, 26, 31, 34-35, 96
Bosch, Juan, 70
Brandt, Willy, 97
Brezhnev, Leonid, 70, 98, 101
Brodie, Bernard, quoted 16-17
Brynes, James, 25, 29
Cambodia, 76, 91
Castro, Fidel, 65-68
Central Intelligence Agency (CIA), 12, 64, 67, 68, 72, 76, 94
Chiang Kai-shek, 39-42; 45, 51
Chile, 71-72
Chinese civil war, 1, 26, 39-49, 42-45
Chou En-lai, 1, 75
Churchill, Winston, 3, 5, 6-7, 9-11, 14, 20, quoted 24, quoted 27-28
Clay, General Lucius, 29
Cominform, 35
Common Market, 34, 50, 98
Communist Party, 22, 23, 33
Containment Doctrine, 30-32, 36-37, 47, 67, 78, 100
Cooper, Chester, quoted 81-82
Council of Foreign Ministers, 14, 24, 25
Cuban missile crisis, 62, 64-71
czarist Russia, 20-21
Czechoslovakia, 4, 35, 97
Dardanelles, 29-30
"Declaration on Liberated Europe," 12

"deterrence," 36
"dialectical materialism," 21
Diem, Ngo Dinh, 76-78, 82
Dien Bien Phu, 75
Dominican Republic, 70-71
domino theory, 78
Dulles, John Foster, 25, 51, 58, 63, 75, 76
Eden, Anthony, 7, 41, 59
Egypt, 58-59
Eisenhower, Dwight D., 43, 50-52, 54, 57, 59, 60, 75, 78
European Economic Community (EEC), 34, 60, 98
European Security Conference, 97-98
Ford, Gerald, R., 93, 98
Four Policemen, 6, 13, 40
France, 13, 25, 58, 59, 75
Fulbright, J. William, quoted 71, 83
Geneva Agreements, 75-76, 77
Geneva Summit meeting, 54
Germany, East, 6, 56, 57, 61, 97; Nazi, 4, 5, 9, 10, 14, 25, 29, 97; West, 29, 35, 56, 59
Goldwater, Barry, 83
Good Neighbor Policy, 62-63, 64, 66
Grand Alliance, 4, 5
Great Britain, 5, 32, 58-59, 98
Greece, 31-32
Guatemala, 64
Guevara, Ernesto "Che," 65-66
Hiroshima, 15
Ho Chi Minh, 74-76
Humphrey, Hubert, 91
Hungary, 56
India, 39
Iran, 58
"Iron Curtain" speech, quoted 27-28
Israel, 99
Italy, 5, 60
Jackson, Henry, 37
Japan, 5, 9-10, 96, 98
Johnson, Lyndon, 70 quoted 71, 77, 81
Kennan, George, quoted 27, 29, quoted 30-31, 33, 36, quoted 43, quoted 86-88

Kennedy, John F., 61, 66-70, 81
Kennedy, Robert, 70, 89
Khmer Rouge, 93
Kissinger, Henry, 92-93
Korean war, 38, 45-50, 75
Kosygin, Alexsei, 70
Krushchev, Nikita, 53, 57, 62, 66, 68, 69, 70, 80
Laos, 76
League of Nations, 8, 9, 13
Leahy, Admiral William, 25
Le Duc Tho, 92
Lend Lease Act, 5
Lenin, Vladimir Ilyich, 22-23
limited war concept, 36-37
Lippman, Walter, quoted 31
MacArthur, General Douglas, 47-48, quoted 49, 50
Manchuria, 10, 15, 41, 48
Mao Tse-tung, 1, 2, 39-42, 48, 51, 80
Marshall, General George C., 33, 41
Marshall Plan, 33-34
Marxism-Leninism, 20-24, 40
Marx, Karl, 21-22
McCarthy, Eugene, 89
McCarthy, Joseph, 43
Molotov, V. M., 6, 13, 14, 25, 53
Monroe Doctrine, 63-64
"Mr. X," quoted 30-31
My Lai, 85
Nagasaki, 15
National Security Council (NSC-68), 37, 60
Nazi-Soviet Pact, 4, 5
Netherlands, 39, 60
"Nixon Doctrine," 91
Nixon, Richard M., 1, 2, 45, 50, 90, quoted 95-96, 100-101
North Atlantic Treaty Organization (NATO), 36, 75
nuclear capability, 36, 99, 70
Organization of Petroleum Exporting Countries (OPEC), 99
Pakistan, 39
Pathet Lao, 76
Pearl Harbor, 5, 8
"pentagonal world," 96, 100, 102
Platt Amendment, 64
Poland, 11, 25, 56
Potsdam Conference, 14-15
Quemoy and Matsu, 50-51
Red Army, 4, 5, 26

revolution, American, 19-20, Russian, 21-24
Rhee, Syngman, 46
Ridgway, Matthew B., 50
Roosevelt, Franklin, D., 3, 5, 6, 7, 8, 9, 10, 11, 12, 40, 162
Rusk, Dean, 78, quoted 85-86
Russian ideology, 21-24
Security Council, 46, 59
Sino-Soviet split, 79-81, 97
Southeast Asia Treaty Organization (SEATO), 76
Sphere of influence, American, 5, 6; British, 32, 58-59; Russian, 24, 25, 56
Sputnik, 55
Stalin, Joseph, 3, 4, 5, 7, 9, 10, 11, 12, 14, 15, 23, 25, 26, 28, 29, 35, 53
Strategic Arms Limitations Talks (SALT), 101
Suez Canal crisis, 58-59
Superpowers 3, 36, 55, 57, 61, 62
Taiwan, 42, 45, 51
Tehran Conference, 7, 8, 9, 10
Tet Offensive, 89
Thieu, Nguyen, 84, 92
Third World, 79, 81
Tonkin Gulf, 82, 83, 100
Trotsky, Leon, 7, 23
Truman, Harry S, quoted 12, 13, 14, 15, 25, 28, 30, quoted 32, 36, 37, 38, 46, 47, 49, 50, 75
Turkey, 30, 68, 70
Ulam, Adam, quoted 80
United Nations, 8, 9, 10, 13, 18, 28, 29, 46, 47, 48
Vandenberg, Arthur, 8, 9, 13, 36
Versailles Peace Conference, 6
Viet Cong, 77, 78, 79, 83, 84, 89, 91, 93
Viet Minh, 74-75, 76
Warsaw Pact, 36
Watergate, 94
Westmoreland, General, 88, 89
Wilson, Woodrow, 6
World War I, 8, 9, 10
World War II, 3, 4, 10, 21, 31, 41, 47, 74, 98
Yalta Conference, 3, 9, 10, 11, 12, 13, 15, 41
Yalu River, 43
Yugoslavia, 35
"zero-sun game," 2, 100